DIY FURNITURE

A step-by-step guide

CHRISTOPHER STUART

DIY FURNITURE

A step-by-step guide

CHRISTOPHER STUART

Laurence King Publishing

Published in 2011 by
Laurence King Publishing Ltd
361–373 City Road
London EC1V 1LR

Reprinted 2012, 2013, 2014

e-mail: enquiries@laurenceking.com
www.laurenceking.com

A catalogue record for this book is available
from the British Library.

ISBN: 978-1-85669-742-2

Design: TwoSheds Design
Senior editor: Peter Jones

Printed in China

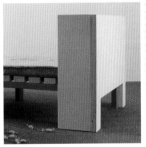

1.
TABLES AND DESKS

Kick back and enjoy your favourite magazine, write something or eat dinner while sipping an ice-cooled drink. Just don't forget those faithful objects that serve them up to you. Their function is simple: to create a surface to hold things and elevate them to a useful height. The myth is that, only here for support, they should do so quietly.

In this chapter are seven designs that speak up. They are unconventional in materials, process and design and refuse to speak quietly. These designers hail from different parts of the world, but all speak the same language: resourceful design. Common industrial materials like PVC, plumbing pipe, wooden dowels, concrete, Styrofoam and windows have been recontextualized to serve you in a less quiet way. These designs go beyond a place for a conversation and become the conversation piece itself.

Adapt the design The table can work as two separate tables or as one large table with two units put together. Create a tiered version with the longer tubes running through two or more levels.

NEWSPAPER TABLE

MALAFOR

The idea behind the Newspaper Table is to create a unique experience for readers. Typically, tables have a flat surface to place items on, with magazines and newspapers usually stacked or hidden on a shelf below. This table was created especially for periodicals and presents them to the user in an innovative way. Unlike a stack where only the top one is visible, the many holders of the Newspaper Table allow the user to display more than one favourite magazine. The colours, images and graphics from each periodical become elements for the user to arrange, allowing them to complete the design.

Black PVC pipes are used to carry water from one place to another, so perhaps it's fitting that they are here re-purposed to bring information to the reader. A simple cylinder pipe is cut at two lengths to form the legs and newspaper holders. The curves of the pipes naturally nestle into each other and are permanently held together with PVC glue and a rubber strap. The process is repeated to create the desired shape. The Newspaper Table was last exhibited at the 'dizajn = designs' exhibition at the Polish Institute in Berlin in 2009.

The same principle of PVC pipes and cargo straps is used to form the bookshelf on page 46.

You will need:

Materials

_ Black plastic water pipe, 77mm diameter, 8m long

_ Rubber strap, 6mm wide, 2.5m long

_Strong PVC glue

Tools

_Hacksaw

_Drill with 6mm bit

1

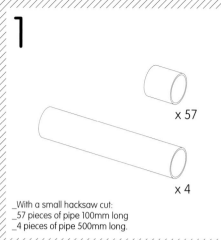

x 57

x 4

_With a small hacksaw cut:
_57 pieces of pipe 100mm long
_4 pieces of pipe 500mm long.

2

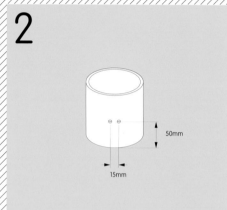

50mm

15mm

_Drill two 6mm holes on one of the short pieces of pipe.

3

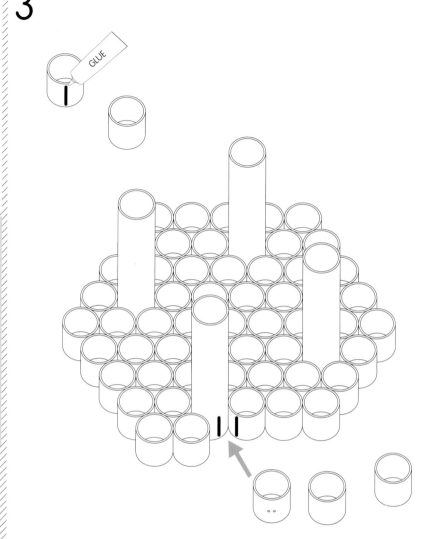

GLUE

_Starting from the centre, glue the pipes together
as in the drawing.

4

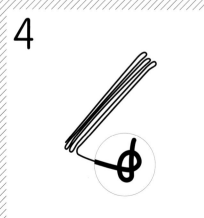

_Tie a knot in the rubber strap.

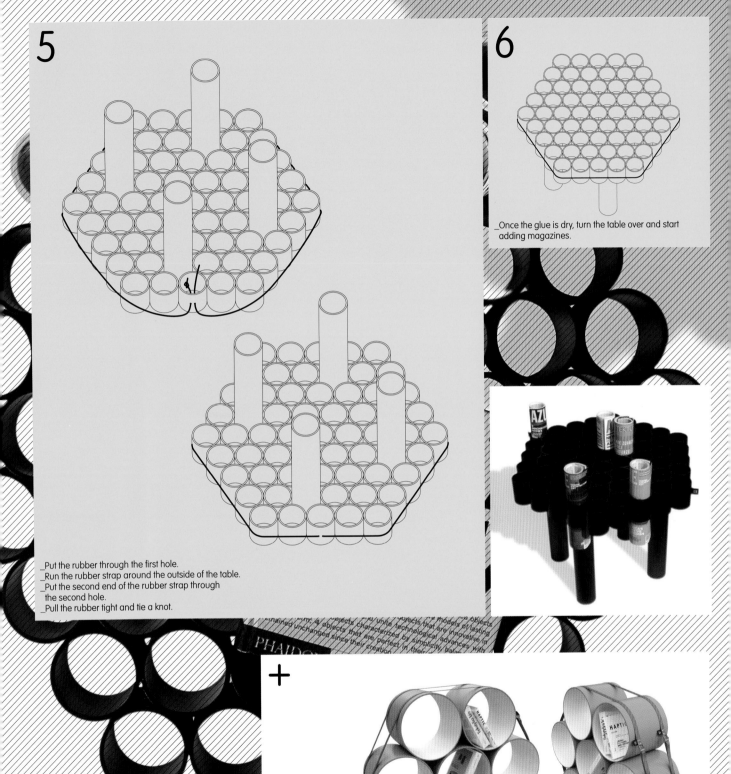

5

_Put the rubber through the first hole.
_Run the rubber strap around the outside of the table.
_Put the second end of the rubber strap through the second hole.
_Pull the rubber tight and tie a knot.

6

_Once the glue is dry, turn the table over and start adding magazines.

+

_Alternatively, make shelves (see page 46).

ULTRA-CONDUCTIVE TABLE

PAUL LOEBACH

This side table grew out of Paul Loebach's Himmeli lighting collection, in which the lights are constructed using tied aluminium tubes. The lights were originally inspired by traditional Scandinavian Christmas crafts made of tied straws. These tied-straw crafts are found in many other countries too.

From this tradition comes the Ultra-Conductive Table. The table was originally designed for a special exhibition 'McMasterpieces' in New York City, in which every object in the show was to be made from raw parts ordered from the American classic McMaster-Carr hardware catalogue. The design's strong structural framework relies on the basic principal of triangulation, in which the negative space of each intersection of tubes forms a triangle. This triangular structure gives the table a crystalline appearance that plays off the shiny copper material and creates a surprisingly strong and stable form.

You will need:

Materials

_ Alloy 101 ultra-conductive copper tubing, 22mm diameter, 8.76m long

_ About 50 large cable ties

_ Sheet of 10mm thick toughened glass measuring 355 x 355mm

Tools

_ Pipe cutter

1

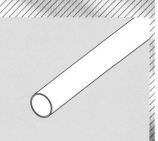

_Using a pipe cutter, cut the copper tubing to the following lengths:
_Four x 279.5mm (part A)
_Four x 470mm (part B)
_Four x 343mm (part C)
_Four x 356mm (part D)
_Four x 216mm (part E)
_Four x 525mm (part F).

2

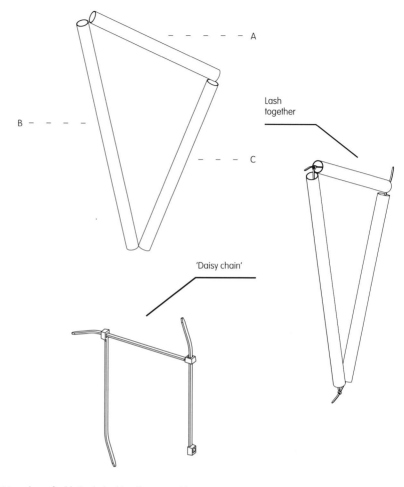

A

B

C

Lash together

'Daisy chain'

_Using a loop of cable ties lashed together, assemble parts A, B and C, as shown. 'Daisy chain' the ties together as needed.
_Make a total of four triangles, each made up of parts A, B and C.

3

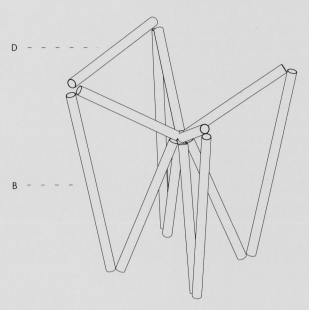

D - - -

B - - -

_Create four loops through each of the top sections,
adding the top pieces (parts D).

4

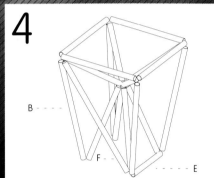

B - - -

F - - - - - - E

_Create four loops through each of the bottom
sections and add the lower pieces (parts E).
_Create four loops through each of the diagonal
sections and add the diagonal pieces (parts F).

5

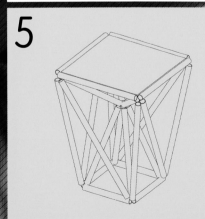

_Set glass on top and enjoy!

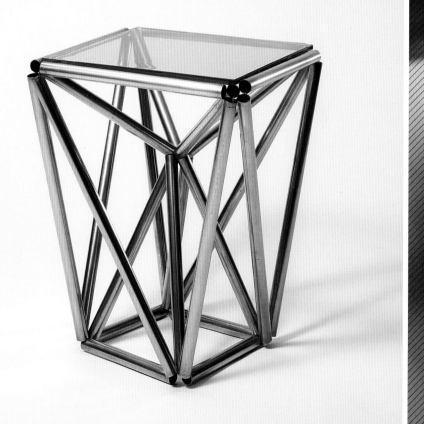

NESTING/ STACKING TABLES

FLORIAN KRÄUTLI

This design was originally intended as an expandable table. The idea was to create something that could be transformed from tall and narrow, to low and wide, like a ball of clay that you can mould tall or press flat. The designer tried an elaborate solution experimenting with cardboard models as well as computer simulations. All the results were too complicated and not very elegant. The current design solves the problem by forming a high table by just stacking several small tables on top of each other, and a low and wide table by placing them next to each other.

The tables are almost like building bricks and invite you to experiment with different configurations. To make this possible without back pain, they have to be very light and are constructed out of a hollow shell with sheets of insulation material for stability. But you could also use a honeycombed cardboard structure or rotation-moulded plastic as a base material. Feel free to experiment!

You will need:

Materials

_One and a half sheets of MDF, 4 x 1220 x 2440mm

_ Four sheets of insulation Styrofoam 32 x 500 x 1000mm (you can also glue two 16mm thick pieces together using Styrofoam glue or white glue)

_One sheet of insulation Styrofoam 12 x 500 x 1000mm

_Wood glue

_Tape (to hold the pieces together while drying)

Tools

_Saw (table saw is ideal)

_Sharp knife or saw (to cut the Styrofoam)

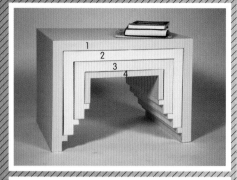

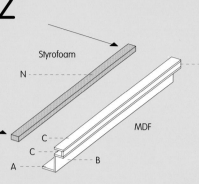

1

_Cut the MDF to the following sizes (see the image above for the numbers of the different tables):

For the feet
_Six x 492 x 32mm (part A)
_Six x 492 x 40mm (part B)
_Twelve x 492 x 24mm (part C)
_Eight x 492 x 12mm (part D)
_Twelve x 20 x 20mm (part E)

For table 1
_Two x 492 x 340mm (part 1F)
_One x 492 x 528mm (part 1G)
_Four x 400 x 40mm (part 1H)
_Two x 600 x 36mm (part 1I)
_Two x 492 x 436mm (part 1J)
_One x 600 x 500mm (part 1K)

For table 2
_Two x 492 x 239mm (part 2F)
_One x 492 x 446mm (part 2G)
_Four x 299 x 40mm (part 2H)
_Two x 518 x 36mm (part 2I)
_Two x 492 x 335mm (part 2J)
_One x 518 x 500mm (part 2K)

For table 3
_Two x 492 x 138mm (part 3F)
_One x 492 x 364mm (part 3G)
_Four x 198 x 40mm (part 3H)
_Two x 436 x 36mm (part 3I)
_Two x 492 x 234mm (part 3J)
_One x 500 x 436mm (part 3K)

For table 4
_Two x 492 x 117mm (part 4F)
_One x 492 x 322mm (part 4G)
_Four x 117 x 20mm (part 4H)
_Two x 354 x 16mm (part 4I)
_Two x 492 x 133mm (part 4J)
_One x 500 x 354mm (part 4K).

_Cut the Styrofoam to the following sizes:
_Two x 492 x 400 x 32mm (part 1L)
_One x 492 x 592 x 32mm (part 1M)
_Two x 492 x 299 x 32mm (part 2L)
_One x 492 x 510 x 32mm (part 2M)
_Two x 492 x 198 x 32mm (part 3L)
_One x 492 x 428 x 32mm (part 3M)
_Two x 492 x 117 x 12mm (part 4L)
_One x 492 x 346 x 12mm (part 4M)
_Six x 492 x 20 x 12mm (part N).

2

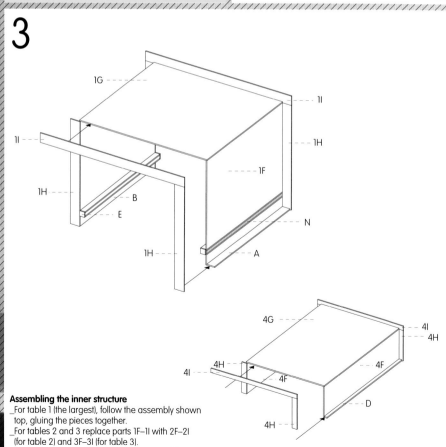

Styrofoam

N

D

C
C

A
B

MDF

Assembling the feet
_ The build process is the same for tables 1, 2 and 3 (the three larger tables).
_Use wood glue to stick together MDF parts A, B, C, D. Parts E are for the small covering ends.
_Strengthen the structure and keep it lightweight by adding Styrofoam part N to fill the void.
_Use tape to hold the pieces in place while they dry.
_Repeat, making six feet in total.

3

Assembling the inner structure
_For table 1 (the largest), follow the assembly shown top, gluing the pieces together.
_For tables 2 and 3 replace parts 1F–1I with 2F–2I (for table 2) and 3F–3I (for table 3).
_For table 4 (the smallest), follow the assembly shown bottom.

4

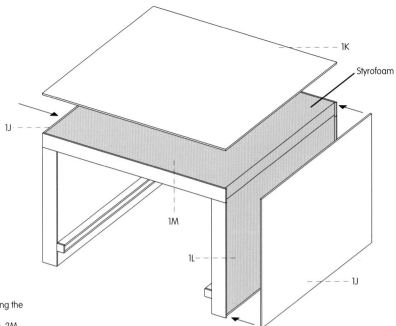

1K

Styrofoam

1J

1M

1L

1J

Assembling the outer structure
_For table 1, follow the assembly shown here, gluing the pieces together.
_For tables 2, 3 and 4, replace parts 1J–1M with 2J–2M (for table 2), 3J–3M (for table 3) and 4J–4M (for table 4).

5

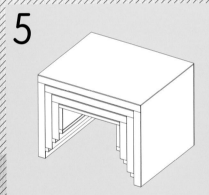

_Nest, stack and then experiment with different configurations.

RESILIENCE TABLE

JULIA LOHMANN

Designed in response to a brief set by the Design Miami/Basel design fair, this table made of concrete and wool was based on the designer's research into man-made structures that are exposed to the elements, re-conquered by nature or demolished by humans.The table reverses the qualities we normally associate with man-made and natural materials. The designer wanted to let the wool and concrete 'dance with one another, and through their interaction reveal their unexpected strengths and weaknesses'.

To make the table she cast concrete, which we normally think of as a strong, structural and long-lasting material, in a flat panel shape and, while still wet, pressed a woollen rug into the material. Massaging the liquid concrete into the fibres bonded the two materials together.

Then, turning destructive force into a creative tool and using the 'undesirable' effects of decay as a design feature, she broke up the shapes when the concrete had almost completely set. The wool, normally seen as organic and transient, now shows its strength, holding the cracked panel together.

The next step was to reconfigure the fragmented concrete and wool panel into a usable three-dimensional form, i.e. that of a bridge-like table, and then to stabilize it. She did this by applying a second coat of concrete to the underside of the table.

The 'Resilience' process allows the creation of a wide range of unique objects based on shapes cast in a single mould. For another concrete piece, see page 112.

You will need:

Materials

_ Fine-grain concrete mix (such as Jesmonite), approx. 150 litres

_Scrap wood, large and small pieces

_Shaggy woollen rug

_Wire mesh or fibreglass netting (optional)

_Plasticine (to waterproof the mould)

_Paper (for model)

Tools

_Several clamps, allow one for every 60mm

_Strong shearing scissors to cut carpet

_Hammer

_Wooden or metal rod to break the concrete

You will also need a flat surface larger than your table to which you can clamp the frame.

1

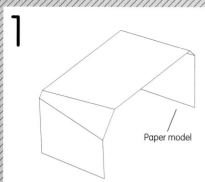

Paper model

_Make a 1:10 paper model of the table design you want.
_Ensure that your breaks total an approximate right
  angle. This will ensure the table is stable.

2

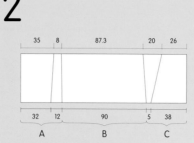

35	8	87.3	20	26

32	12	90	5	38
A		B		C

_Flatten the paper and mark on the folds.
_Take measurements of the paper and scale them
  up x 10.

3

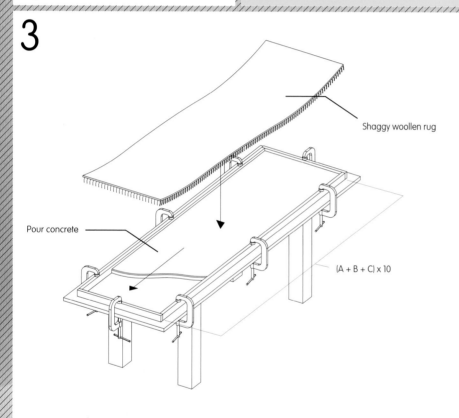

Shaggy woollen rug

Pour concrete

(A + B + C) x 10

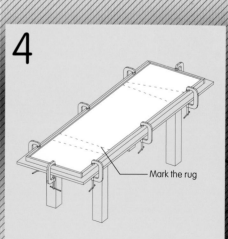

_Find or cut a smooth flat surface slightly larger than your table.
_Make a mould by cutting lengths of wood about 20mm deep and attaching
  them to the flat surface with clamps or screws.
_Waterproof the mould with plasticine by rubbing it into the cracks. Otherwise
  the concrete might spill out.
_Prepare a shaggy woollen rug by cutting it to the shape of your mould. The
  rug will stretch about 20mm on each side when it gets wet, so cut it 20mm
  shorter on each side.
_Mix the concrete and fill your mould to about 20mm deep.
_Knock the wood with a hammer to get all the air bubbles out.
_Massage some wet concrete into the hairs of the rug.
_Carefully place the shaggy rug into the wet concrete, hairs down. Make sure
  the concrete and wool bond well. Massage the rug in and press it down. It
  should sit in the concrete without any air between.
_Now let it dry overnight.

4

Mark the rug

_Mark on the rug where you need to have the cracks
  (using measurements from your model).
_Make sure you do it the right way around. The rug
  side of your table will be the underside.

5

Apply pressure

Bar underneath

Rug side down

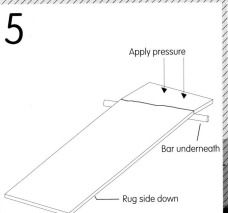

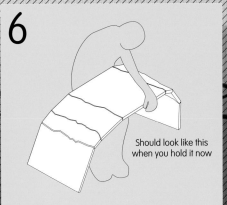

_Remove the table carefully from the mould and turn it over.
_Double check your marks and move the concrete on the flat surface. Handle it carefully as it is very fragile in this state.
_Place a wooden or metal rod underneath the first one of your marks and carefully break the concrete over it, like breaking chocolate from a bar.
_Repeat with the other cracks.

6

Should look like this when you hold it now

_Lift the table to see the other side. If you want more cracks, add them now.

7

Support

Add more concrete

Attach small boards

_Now all you need to do is reinforce your table from the back to make it stand by itself.
_Turn it over and find a way that it can rest in the right position. Build a fixture or place it against other objects to hold it in place.
_Attach more small wooden pieces about 50mm high along the edges of the table to create a new mould.
_Use individual pieces the length of the space between each crack.
_Pour more concrete in and add wire mesh or fibreglass netting to reinforce the shape on the back until it is strong enough to be stable as a table. It should be roughly 50mm in total thickness.

8

_Let it dry and your cracked concrete table is ready to use.

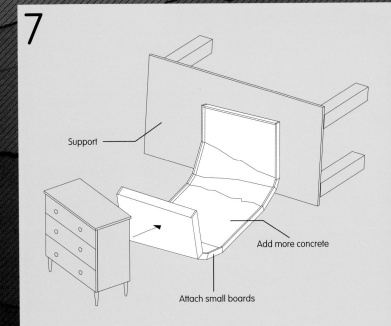

BRASS ENSEMBLE

JORRE VAN AST

This series of ready-made furniture frames for temporary use is made from ramin dowel joined together with the brass compression fittings normally used to connect copper piping in plumbing. The lightness of the frames makes them portable and they are easily assembled and disassembled.

The frames can be used in different formations to create both large and small tables and a long bench. The instructions overleaf are for the long table supports shown opposite top. The surface shown here is Phenolic board, but other surfaces such as an unfinished door blank, strengthened glass or plywood could be used.

Follow the instructions to complete the table and use the learned process to make other things. Perhaps a bench to accompany your new table!

Jorre van Ast studied at the Royal College of Art in London and is part of the OKAY studio which also includes Peter Marigold (see page 38).

You will need:

Materials

_Six wooden dowels, 22mm diameter 2.4m long

_Eight 22mm brass Ts (part A)

_Twelve 22mm brass elbows (part B)

_Phenolic board for table top (shown) 20 x 988 x 1938mm. Other suggestions: Baltic birch plywood, a hollow, unfinished door blank.

Tools

_Cutting pliers

_Saw

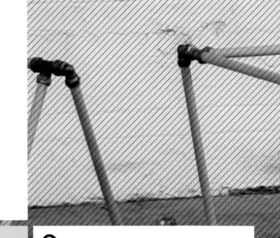

1

_Cut dowels to the following lengths:

_Eight x 800mm (part C)
_Two x 600mm (part D)
_Two x 400mm (part E)
_Two x 350mm (part F)
_Two x 290mm (part G)
_Two x 210mm (part H)
_Two x 150mm (part I)
_Two x 100mm (part J)

2

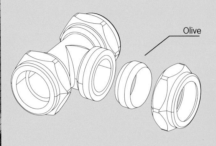

Olive

_Unscrew the brass nut from the fitting and take the copper olive out.

3

3mm

_Using cutting pliers make two cuts in the olive approximately 3mm apart.
_Put the olive back in its original position and loosely screw the nut back on.

4

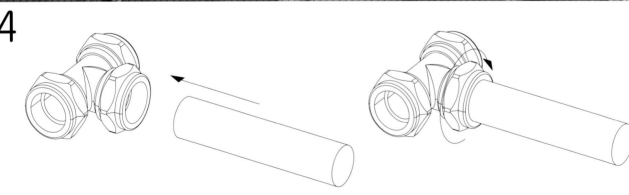

_Insert the dowel into the brass fitting and tighten the nut.

5

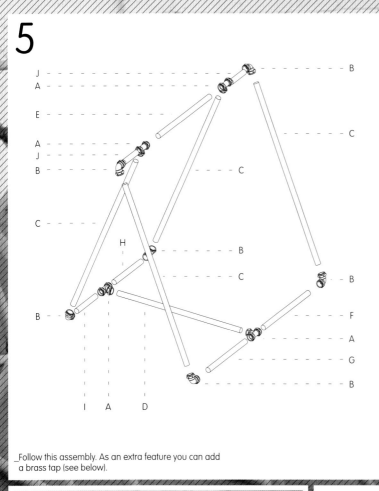

_Follow this assembly. As an extra feature you can add
a brass tap (see below).

6

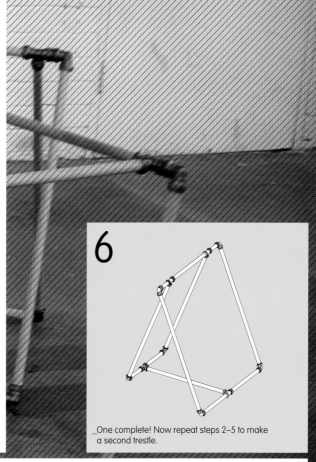

_One complete! Now repeat steps 2–5 to make
a second trestle.

7

_Add the top.
_Using the same build process, experiment and
make other things.

+

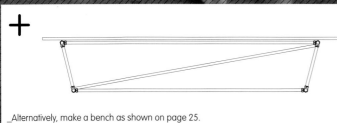

_Alternatively, make a bench as shown on page 25.

KOFITABLE

GABRIELA KOWALSKA OF KOFIKOLEKTIF

This table recycles the kind of plastic windows left behind on the streets once the tide of summer renovation fever has retreated. KOFITABLE is both stable and mobile, perfectly fitting with modern needs.

In the example shown opposite, impregnated oak table legs handcrafted by a master carpenter from Pruszcza in Poland are combined with industrial furniture wheels and one of the many found plastic windows.

A handle, once used for opening the window, now becomes a handle to pull and move the KOFITABLE around. It makes cleaning or rearranging the room much easier, as the table is easily moved but can then be locked in place with the wheel locks. The design makes a virtue of the safety glass used in modern windows, making a piece that is both robust and matched to most interiors.

You will need:

Materials

_Four industrial locking casters, 50mm diameter with top mounting plate (40 x 40mm)

_Four wooden legs of your choice. They will need a 60 x 60mm square (not a circle) at both top and bottom ends. Suggested height 650mm.

_Window 1200 x 760mm with handle. We recommend a standard single-pane, plastic, double-glazed window without divided segments.

_Eight L-shaped metal brackets, 30 x 30 x 30mm

_32 screws, 5 x 25mm (part F)

_Four hanger bolts, 12 x 35mm (part C)

Tools

_Screwdriver

_Drill

_Marker

_Pencil

_File (optional)

1

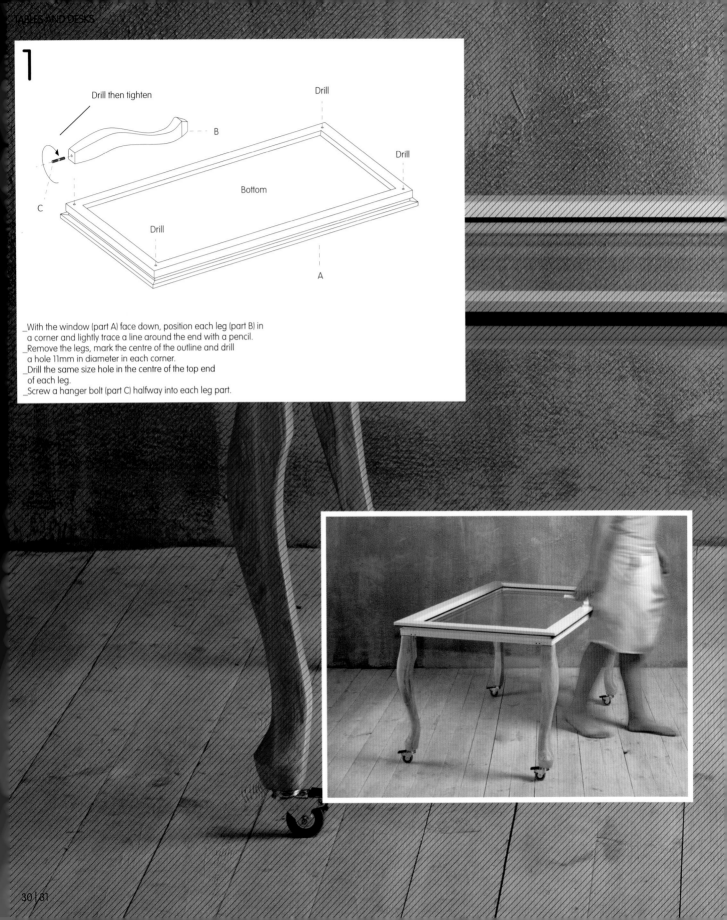

Drill then tighten

Drill

B

Drill

C

Bottom

Drill

Drill

A

_With the window (part A) face down, position each leg (part B) in
  a corner and lightly trace a line around the end with a pencil.
_Remove the legs, mark the centre of the outline and drill
  a hole 11mm in diameter in each corner.
_Drill the same size hole in the centre of the top end
  of each leg.
_Screw a hanger bolt (part C) halfway into each leg part.

2

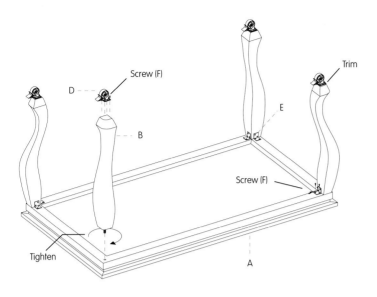

D
Screw (F)
B
Trim
E
Screw (F)
Tighten
A

_Attach each leg to the window by screwing the other end of the hanger bolt into the hole.
_Place two L-shaped brackets on the insides of the leg where the leg meets the window and mark the holes with a fine-pointed marker.
_Twist the legs off from the window and drill 4mm holes where your marks are.
_Attach the legs again and attach the brackets with screws (parts F).
_Predrill holes for the casters (D) and secure with screws (F). You may need to trim the edge of the metal plate with a file.

3

_Turn over the table and wheel it away!

WRITING DESK

LUIGI FUMAGALLI FOR RECESSION DESIGN

The Writing Desk is made entirely of wood. It recalls the secretaires of traditional furniture but its styling is inspired by pieces from the 1950s and 1960s. It has a simple design: a table top and a structure, assembled with screws; everything is made of deal wood, both the panels for the top and the splints, which act as supports.

You can easily buy the materials needed for the design in any DIY store. The designer Luigi Fumagalli is part of the Recession Design group. Their aim is to design 'a collection of objects created using everyday DIY products that are processed and assembled using common utensils and accessories. Featuring a design that is clean but not banal, essential but not meagre, the objects show how a good project can result in high-level design, even with the use of readily available materials and utensils.'

Other Recession Design pieces are featured on pages 68, 76, 92, 108 and 116.

You will need:

Materials

_Sheet of pine 20 x 700 x 2000mm

_Six pine boards 20 x 40 x 1300mm

_Two hinges, 40mm long (part F)
  with small screws

_Pack of screws 3.5mm long

Tools

_Drill

_Saw

1

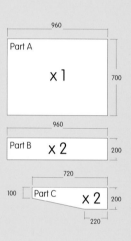

Part A   x 1   (960 × 700)

Part B   x 2   (960 × 200)

Part C   x 2   (720 / 220 / 100 × 200)

_Cut the 700 x 2000mm sheet of wood to the following sizes:

_One x 700 x 960mm (part A)
_Two x 960 x 200mm (part B)
_Two x 720 x 200mm, with slant cut as shown (part C).

2

Part D   x 4   1300

Part E   x 2   1080

_Cut the 20 x 40mm boards to the following lengths:

_Four x 1300mm long (part D)
_Two x 1080mm long (part E).

3

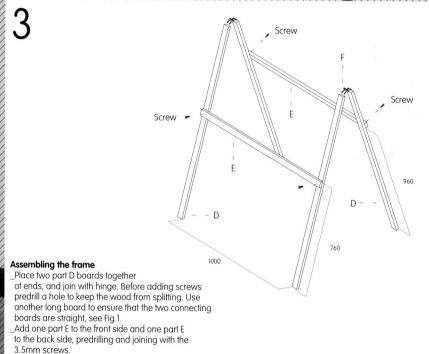

Assembling the frame
_Place two part D boards together
at ends, and join with hinge. Before adding screws predrill a hole to keep the wood from splitting. Use another long board to ensure that the two connecting boards are straight, see Fig.1.
_Add one part E to the front side and one part E to the back side, predrilling and joining with the 3.5mm screws.

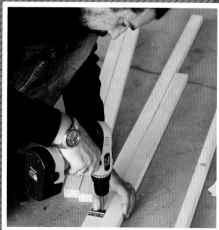

4

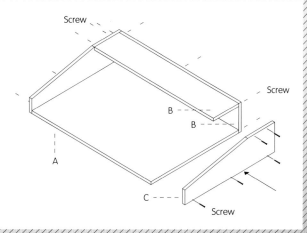

Assembling the box

_Predrill holes and screw together. You will need three screws along the bottom of the sides and two where it meets the top. There are six screws along the back: three along the top and three along the bottom.

5

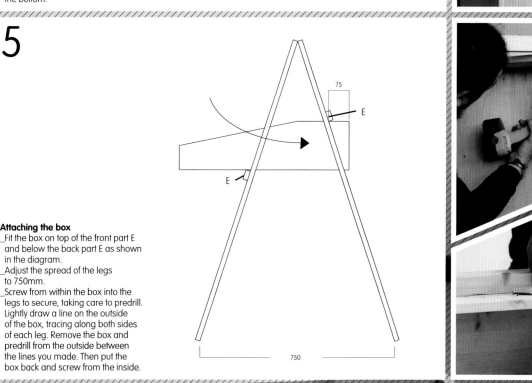

Attaching the box

_Fit the box on top of the front part E and below the back part E as shown in the diagram.
_Adjust the spread of the legs to 750mm.
_Screw from within the box into the legs to secure, taking care to predrill. Lightly draw a line on the outside of the box, tracing along both sides of each leg. Remove the box and predrill from the outside between the lines you made. Then put the box back and screw from the inside.

6

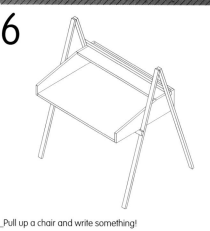

_Pull up a chair and write something!

2. STORAGE

Don't toss that wood in the fire just yet! Your wall longs for the sprawling trapezoids of the Split Box Shelves. Or maybe triangles are your aesthetic. We have that covered too. Whether you dwell in a humbly sized abode or a space fit for a gallery, the modular shelving designs in this chapter will expand and contract to fit any sized living space. And if you're short of glue or wary of woodwork, you're in luck because zip ties and bolts are the preferred securing method here.

For the purists out there, we haven't forgotten about you. Wood never looked so good as it does in the minimally shaped Box Sideboard. All the objects in this chapter are so beautiful they look good with or without anything on them.

SPLIT BOX SHELVES

PETER MARIGOLD

The Split series is based on the simple geometric principle that the angles of a split form will always total 360 degrees, irregular, yet always perfectly complete. Peter Marigold applied this principle to working with simple small logs by dividing the logs into pieces cutting random angles and then using them as the corners for small crates.

The first of the Split series were the Split Box Shelves, where the small, irregular crates are joined to each other and fastened to the wall. The sprawling geometric structure that results appears to be both chaotic and logical, the units taking on a cell-like presence. Marigold was captivated by the idea that any one of the boxes could have been contained inside any of the logs. It therefore follows that an infinite number of possible boxes could exist inside the piece of wood. The resulting wall installation is an expression of the phenomenon of the infinite existing inside any point that we observe.

The Split Box Shelves were first installed as part of the Great Brits exhibition at the Milan Salone di Mobili 2007, then a larger display was made for the Paul Smith showroom in Milan. Then an ongoing performance took place at Design Miami 2007 where local avocado and mango trees were used to create a limited-edition set of the boxes.

Peter Marigold is part of OKAY studio, along with Jorre van Ast (page 24).

You will need:

Materials

_Stock of either kiln-dried or air-dried logs (if they are not dried, the units will warp in the future)

_Different length strips of 6–9mm thick plywood (for heavier shelves use 9mm)

_A piece of scrap wood a little larger than the diameter of logs for the 'v' jig

_Small nails or brad nailing gun

_Threaded bolt 4mm diameter with nut (the length should be about twice as thick as the plywood, plus room for the nut)

Tools

_Hammer

_Saw (bandsaw recommended)

1

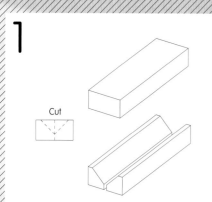

Cut

_Cut the scrap wood into a v shape and then cut this in half. This will be your jig to help secure the logs when cutting.

2

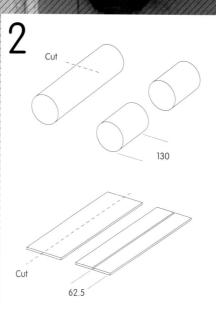

Cut

130

Cut

62.5

_Using the saw, cut the logs into 130mm lengths (use completely DRY LOGS as wet will damage your saw).
_Cut the plywood into long strips 62.5mm wide (you will cut further different lengths later).

3

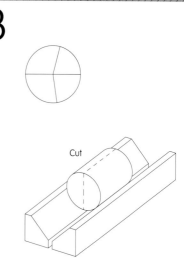

Cut

_Place the logs on the v jig and saw them in half. Be very careful as the logs are irregular shapes and can easily flip into the blade.
_Then take each half and cut it in two parts. Experiment with the angles; the angle will determine the shape of each box – see below.

4

B C
A D

B C
A D

B C
A D

B

C

A

D

_Turn each of the four wedges around. Each wedge will make a straight line with its neighbour.
_Spread out the wedges as far as you like to create the box corners. The farther apart you move the wedges, the bigger the box.

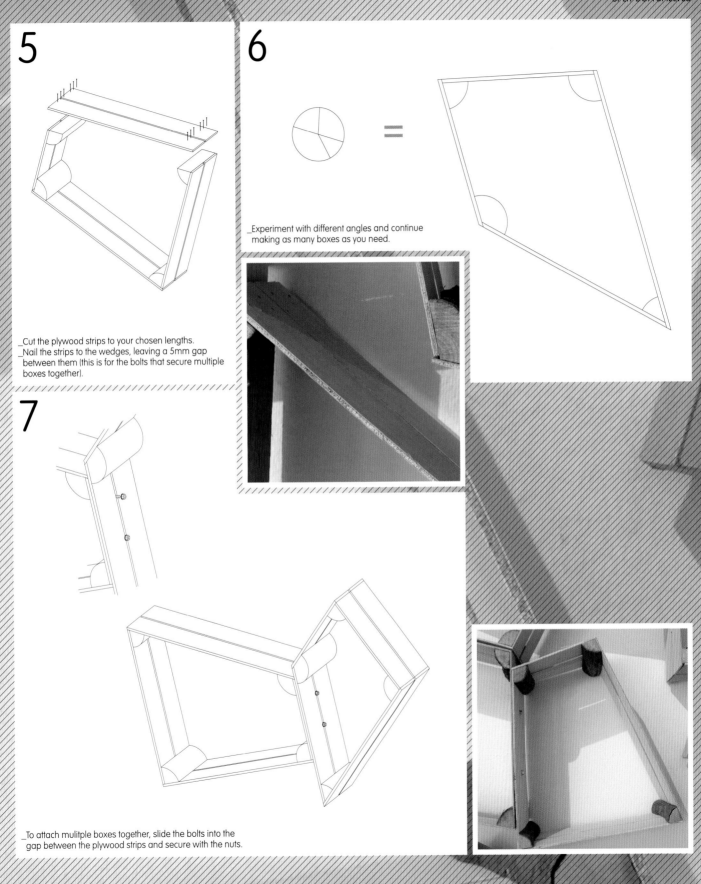

5

_Cut the plywood strips to your chosen lengths.
_Nail the strips to the wedges, leaving a 5mm gap
between them (this is for the bolts that secure multiple
boxes together).

6

=

_Experiment with different angles and continue
making as many boxes as you need.

7

_To attach mulitple boxes together, slide the bolts into the
gap between the plywood strips and secure with the nuts.

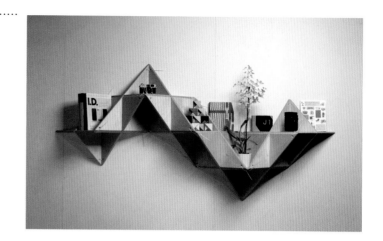

T.SHELF

JAE WON CHO OF J1STUDIO

T.SHELF is an abbreviation for Triangle Shelf, a shelving system that can be set up around your existing furniture, adding storage space to what you already have, or it can hang by itself on a wall as a sculptural object. Assembled from two triangular modules, the T.SHELF_system uses zip ties to tie triangles into one piece of solid furniture/sculpture and functions as a display for books, magazines, plants, pictures or anything you want.

The concept was to create a piece that is easy to set up anywhere and pack flat for space saving transportation but without losing the quality of the design. 'My first approach was to get rid of screws, which also gets rid of the tools needed to assemble the furniture,' says Jae Won Cho (aka J1), designer of the T.SHELF_system and the principal of J1studio. This led to using a traditional slot-joint technique and triangular panels with the structure integrated in the shape.

'I chose the most common material that can replace the screws and do the same job,' says Jae Won Cho. Rather than producing more parts for the furniture, the T.SHELF_system uses zip ties, a ready-made industrial material for tying electrical cables. T.SHELF uses a numbering system that indicates how many triangles to use. It is available in sets of eight triangles and zip ties (T8) with an instruction book that shows five different configurations. Made in Los Angeles using CNC technique, it can be delivered in four weeks' time.

You will need:

Materials

_Sheet of plywood 6 x 1220 x 1220mm

_Pack of cable ties

_Two pieces of wood, 50 x 50 x 230mm (part C)

_A few screws for mounting to the wall

Tools

_Saw

_Chisel

_Mallet

_Drill

_Countersink bit

1

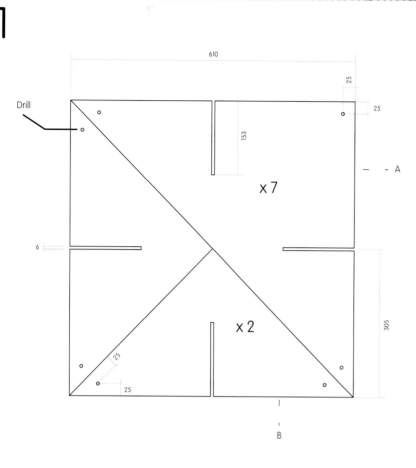

Drill

610

25

25

153

x 7

6

- A

305

x 2

25

25

B

_With the saw cut the plywood sheet to make a piece 610 x 610mm.
_Diagonally cut the square into two large triangles, making part A.
_To make part B divide again into two small triangles. You will need
 seven pieces of part A and two pieces of part B.
_Use the saw, chisel and mallet to cut out 6mm slots. Each part A has
 two slots; each part B has one slot.
_Drill 6mm holes as shown. Each part A has three holes; each part B
 has two holes. Add a chamfer to the hole with a countersink bit to
 soften the edge.

2

A

A

B

_To assemble place one triangle (A) perpendicular to
 the floor and join a second triangle (A) by sliding into
 place using the slots
_Add one triangle (B) on the opposite side.

3

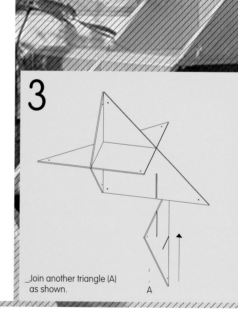

_Join another triangle (A)
 as shown.

A

4

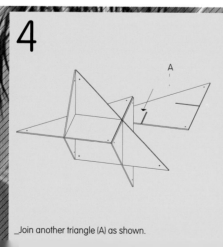

A

_Join another triangle (A) as shown.

5

A

_Join another triangle (A) as shown.

6

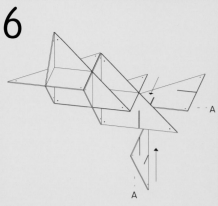

_Repeat steps 3 and 4.

7

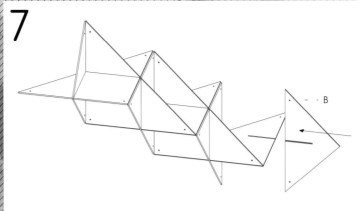

_Close the piece by slotting in triangle (B) as shown.

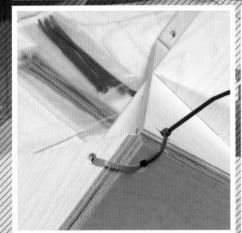

8

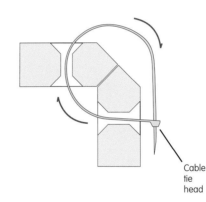

Cable tie head

_After joining all the triangles, connect them together using cable ties.
_Position the cable tie head on the outside for a tighter hold: the inside corner will tend to be looser.

9

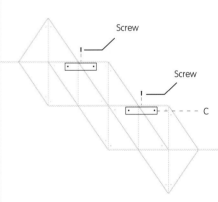

Screw

Screw

C

_Position the T.SHELF on the wall and mark two lines on the right side of the top shelf and middle shelf.
_Mount two wood pieces (parts C) on the line, aligning them on the right.
_Place the T.SHELF on the brackets and secure with screws from the top.

10

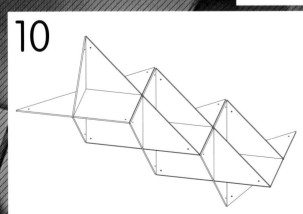

_Now fill with your favourite objects.

+

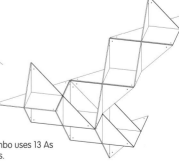

This floor-standing form uses three As and two Bs.

This combo uses 13 As and 4 Bs.

_Here are some other designs you can make.

PIPE LINE SHELF

MALAFOR

Partner piece to the Newspaper Table (see page 8), the Pipe Line Shelf was exhibited at the Colour Days exhibition in Warsaw in 2007. One of the simplest pieces in the book, it can nevertheless be combined with multiple units to form a unique, stacking shelving system.

The Polish design duo state: 'We started by creating objects that we could produce in short bursts (such as Newspaper Table and Pipe Line Shelf). Now, we are also working on projects for the industrial design of its own brand, such as Active Basket – shopping baskets for people in wheelchairs. We also design household projects commissioned by external companies.'

You will need:

Materials

_PVC pipe, 300mm diameter, 2.1m long

_Two lashing straps, 25mm wide, 4m long with clips

_Paint for tubes (optional)

Tools

_Saw

1

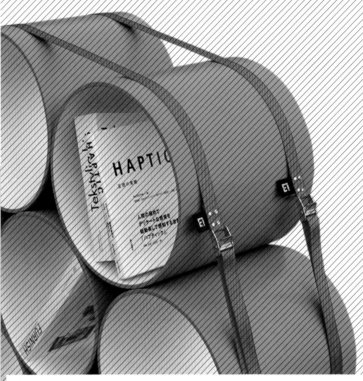

x 7

_Using the saw cut seven pieces of pipe 300mm long.

2

_Position the pipes on the floor.
_Wrap the straps around the pipes.
_Pull the straps through the clips and tighten.

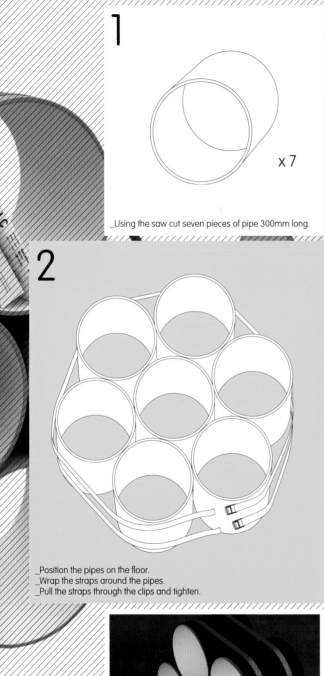

3

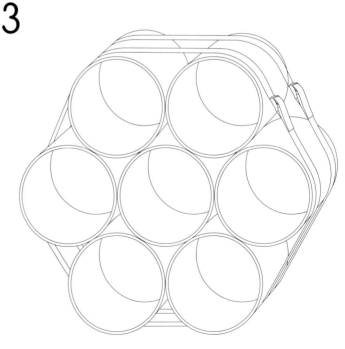

_Stand the bookcase up and fill with books.

BOX SIDEBOARD

WILLIAM GITTINS

This elegant sideboard was designed to be as simple a piece of storage as possible, one that was both generic and bold. The designer was inspired by the plank construction of a recovered sixteenth-century coffer, and also influenced by the form of long cardboard boxes that he had seen on the streets of Colombia.

Gittins felt that the first piece he designed was wrong: the proportions were too heavy. However, this led to a commission that offered a chance element leading to a second design. This design was made from teak, one of only two woods certified as sustainable.

Parallel to working on the sideboard, the designer was working on a project using randomly generated numbers to break cycles of patterns. The element of chance, integral and unnoticeable but with a sequential impact beyond us, allowed him to stand back and address obstacles on the project from another perspective.

You will need:

Materials

_Sheet of plywood 9 x 374 x 1824mm

_21 wood boards 18 x 100 x 1850mm

_Wood board 24 x 100 x 650mm

_Nails and screws

_Eight Euro-style overlay hinges

Tools

_Saw

_Hammer

_Drill

_Mallet

_Countersink bit

_PVA glue

1

Top, bottom, back

Notch detail

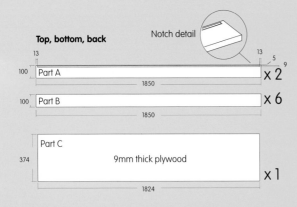

100 | Part A | x 2
13 ... 1850 ... 13 | 5 | 9

100 | Part B | x 6
1850

374 | Part C
9mm thick plywood
1824 | x 1

Legs

Part D x 2
65 | 352

24mm thick

x 2
100 | Part E | 40 | Part F x 2
250 | 64

Cutting the boards for the top, bottom, back and legs
_All the boards are 18mm thick except part C,
which is 9mm plywood, and parts E and F, which
are 24mm thick.
_Cut 5mm deep x 9mm wide notches along the
lengths of parts A, 5mm from the edge. Leave 13mm
on each side.

2

Side, centre & shelf

Part G | 100 | 364 | x 9

Part H | 50 | 363 | x 10

Part I | 25 | 363 | x 2

notch detail

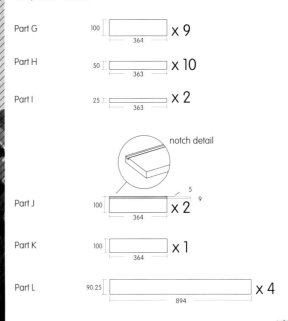

Part J | 100 | 364 | x 2 | 5 | 9

Part K | 100 | 364 | x 1

Part L | 90.25 | 894 | x 4

Doors

Part M | 461
100 | 150 | x 2 | 13

Part N | 461
100 | 150 | x 2

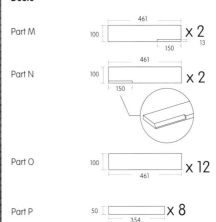

Part O | 100 | 461 | x 12

Part P | 50 | 354 | x 8

Cutting the boards for the sides, centre, shelf and doors
_Use 18mm thick boards for all the pieces.
_For part J, cut a 9mm wide x 5mm deep notch the length
of the board (364mm). Make sure the top of the notch
is spaced 5mm from the top edge of the board.
_Cut a 45-degree bevel 150mm wide on parts M and N.
Note that they are on opposite sides of the cut pieces
(forming the left and right doors).

3

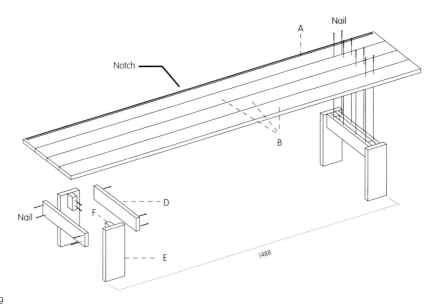

Assembling the legs and bottom

_Nail together two parts each of D, E, F to create one leg assembly. Stagger the nails so they don't hit each other when nailing the opposite side.

_Repeat to make a second leg assembly and space the two legs 1488mm apart.

_Attach three part B boards to the leg assembly by nailing through the top.

_Attach one part A board with the notch facing up and to the back.

4

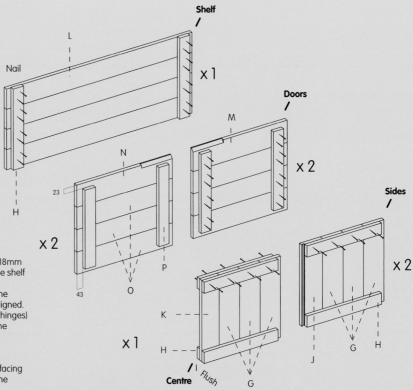

Assembling the shelf, doors, sides and centre

_Lay four part L boards flat and nail two part H pieces across 18mm from each end to make a shelf. The 18mm is the space for the shelf support.

_Lay three part O boards flat with a part N at the top. Ensure the bevel is facing up. Nail on two parts P, keeping the boards aligned. The spacing here is 43mm on the sides (space to mount the hinges) and 23mm on the top (space to clear the top when closing the door). Repeat so that you have made two right-hand doors.

_Repeat the above step, using two parts M to make two left-hand doors.

_Use parts G, J and H to make two sides; ensure the notch is facing outwards (align the edge of parts H with the inside edge of the notch).

_To make the centre panel, sandwich three part G boards and one part K board between four part H cross pieces. Nail together, ensuring that the H and K boards align flush at the ends.

5

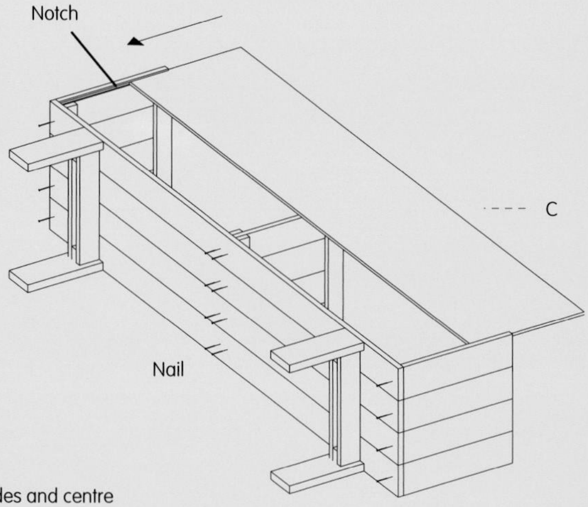

Notch

C

Nail

_Lay the base on its front and nail the sides and centre of the bottom into parts H, making sure that the notches are facing inwards and are aligned with each other.
_Apply some glue to the sides and bottom edges of the plywood (part C) and slide into place. Wipe away any excess glue while it is still wet.

6

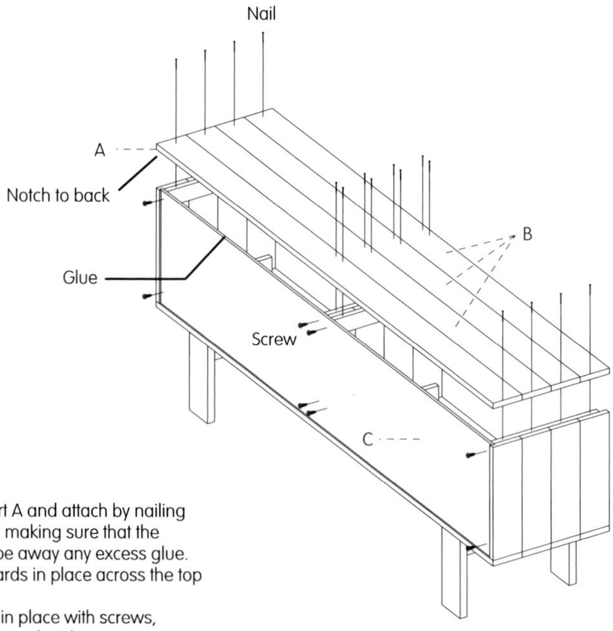

Nail

A

Notch to back

B

Glue

Screw

C

_Apply glue to the notch of part A and attach by nailing from the top through parts H, making sure that the plywood sits in the notch. Wipe away any excess glue.
_Nail the remaining part B boards in place across the top of the sideboard.
_Fix the plywood back (part C) in place with screws, predrilling and countersinking so that the screws sit flush.

7

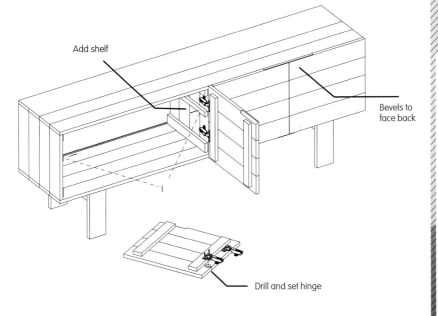

Add shelf

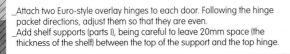

Bevels to
face back

Drill and set hinge

_Attach two Euro-style overlay hinges to each door. Following the hinge
packet directions, adjust them so that they are even.
_Add shelf supports (parts I), being careful to leave 20mm space (the
thickness of the shelf) between the top of the support and the top hinge.

8

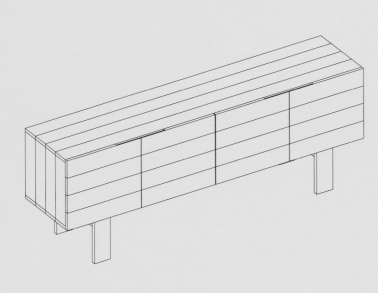

_Fill with drinks and enjoy!

3.
LIGHTING

Each light has its own gesture, which ultimately affects our mood. Some fixtures contain the bulb and let the light slowly fill the room. Others are delicate supports that allow a bare bulb's light to spill into the space. Some are seldom turned on, yet they remain in the house contributing to the environment. They take shape in many forms, but when choosing one, we know the one for us. Its gesture resonates.

The objective of a lamp is firstly to hold a bulb and secondly to control the bulb's light. Its form is influenced by its particular function, but the possibilities are endless. The look is partially determined by the materials used to create the fixture. Although the shape is ultimately determined by the designer, every material presents its own limitations and potential. In this chapter, each designer has explored the use of materials commonly found at building supply stores. They look beyond the standard use of these materials to see how their properties benefit the designs. Hopefully, they inspire you to see things in a different light.

LAMPADA A STELO

KUENG CAPUTO

This simple, oversized anglepoise lamp was created for the 2009 exhibition Autoprogettazione Revisited: Easy-to-Assemble Furniture by Enzo Mari and Invited Guests at the Architecture Association in London. This was a commemoration of the renowned Italian designer's 1974 project for self-made furniture 'Autoprogettazione by Mari'. For the 2009 exhibition nine artists and designers were commissioned to respond to Mari's instruction-based furniture plans with their own set of instructions.

In a text accompanying the instructions, Mari writes that 'anyone, apart from factories and traders, can use the designs to make them by themselves'. The idea of self-fabrication of quality design objects is supported by this lamp in which the position of the arm is adjustable by tying the cord at different lengths.

Kueng Caputo believe that designers' roles are not merely about selling goods, but also about offering ideas and methods that encourage richer daily practice: by exploring alternative sustainable modes of consumption, production and reproduction. They question the traditional relationship between designer/ entrepreneur/public, as consumers are no longer mere recipients of cultural goods. They constantly ask who they design for, exploring how the creativity of designers and consumers can be acknowledged and encouraged.

You will need:

Materials

_Standard light kit with socket with 6m long strong and flexible cord (one with integrated switch on the bulb holder is best)

_Length of wooden dowel 5mm diameter, 120mm long

_Bolt with wingnut, 5mm diameter, 70mm long

_Ten nails or screws (for a cleaner look, use wood screws and countersink the holes)

_Wood board 18 x 60 x 5400mm (Baltic birch plywood recommended).

Tools

_Drill

_Hammer

_Saw

_Screwdriver (optional)

_Countersink bit (optional)

_Wooden mallet

_Staple gun (to fix the cord to the beam)

1

A ▭ 1720mm long

B ▭ 1780mm long

C ▭ 620mm long

D ▭ 620mm long

E ▭ 480mm long

_Cut the board into the following five pieces:
_60 x 18 x 1720mm (part A)
_60 x 18 x 1780mm (part B)
_60 x 18 x 620mm (part C)
_60 x 18 x 620mm (part D)
_60 x 18 x 480mm (part E).

2

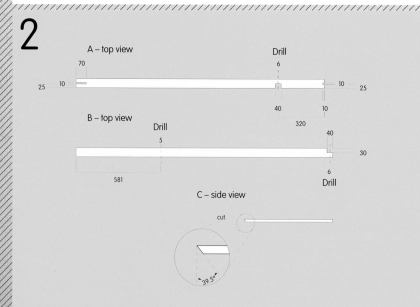

A – top view

70

Drill

6

25   10

10

25

40

10

320

B – top view

Drill

5

40

30

581

6

Drill

C – side view

cut

39.5°

Notch and drill
_Cut a 10 x 70mm notch from one end of part A.
_Cut a 10 x 10mm notch from the other end of part A.
_Measure 320mm from that same end. This will be the centre line for your
  hole and the other notch. Cut a 40 x 30mm notch and drill a 6mm hole
  through the board (A). This is for your bolt.

_Cut a 40 x 30mm notch from the upper right-hand corner of part B.
_Measure 20mm in from the right side and drill a 6mm hole through the
  board. This is for your bolt.
_Measure 581mm in from the left side and drill a 5mm hole through
  part B. This is for your dowel.

_Cut a mitre of 39.5 degrees on one end of board C.

3

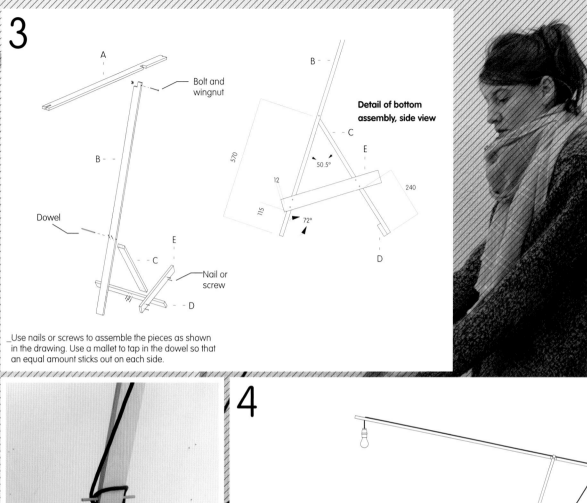

A

Bolt and
wingnut

B

Detail of bottom
assembly, side view

C

E

570

12

50.5°

115

72°

240

Dowel

E

C

D

Nail or
screw

D

_Use nails or screws to assemble the pieces as shown
in the drawing. Use a mallet to tap in the dowel so that
an equal amount sticks out on each side.

4

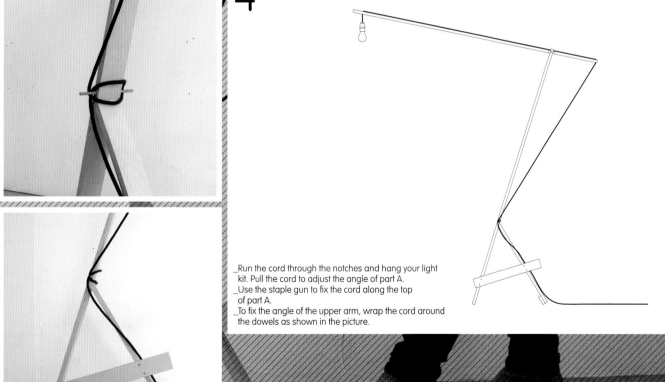

_Run the cord through the notches and hang your light
kit. Pull the cord to adjust the angle of part A.
_Use the staple gun to fix the cord along the top
of part A.
_To fix the angle of the upper arm, wrap the cord around
the dowels as shown in the picture.

YOU MAKE IT CHANDELIER

LINDSEY ADELMAN STUDIO

The You Make It Chandelier is part of a series of lights designed with standard off-the-shelf parts from lighting industry suppliers. Often low-cost design means sacrificing on the quality of materials or construction; the You Make It Chandelier offers an alternative that demands a little more time to assemble in exchange for having a more permanent piece.

For the designer Lindsey Adelman, however, as important as the final product is the sharing of a design method. Lindsey started experimenting with readily available parts before designing the custom hardware she now uses with her Bubble series. This process of exploration is an important part of the way her studio works; they aim to open the larger process of the design up to others by giving a bit of guidance as to suppliers and basic wiring information. As such, the actual configuration of the You Make It Chandelier is offered simply as a starting point; ideally it is approached simply as a suggestion and a kit of parts ripe for manipulation.

Lindsey is based in New York and we have reproduced her recommendations for parts in the list on the right, but if you live outside the US you will need to adapt the materials list to local specifications. The brass pipes, swivels and cluster bodies are fairly universal but you will need to adapt to, and take advice on, local bulb fittings and wiring.

You will need:

Materials

From grandbrass.com

_Plug (part A, item # PL183PBK)

_Length of wire 3657mm (610mm + the distance between the closest plug and the lamp) (part B, item # WI18POG)

_Brass loop (part C, item # LO111)

_Brass pipes, 10mm threaded on both ends, various lengths (parts D):

Two x 178mm (item # PIBR07-0X8)
Three x 76mm (item # PIBR03-0X8)
One x 127mm (item # PIBR05-0X8)
Three x 152mm (item # PIBR06-0X8)
Two x 102mm (item # PIBR04-0X8)

_Three nuts, 4mm thick by 14mm wide (part E, item # NU430)

_One cluster body, 38 x 40mm (part F, item # BOLG3)

_Three brass swivels, 19 x 32mm (part G, item # SV140)

_Two coupling bodies, 13 x 14mm (part H, item # NE449NP)

_Five light sockets, 38 x 52mm (part I, item # SO10045)

_Five candle bulbs (part J, item # BUET10C40)

_One globe bulb (part K, item # BUEG16C40)

_Five slip rings, 9.5mm diameter (part L, item # SRO-3/8NP)

_Five brass cups, 39 x 51mm (part M, item # CU578)

_Three brass cluster bodies, 21 x 29mm (part N, item # BOT2)

_Two steel nipples, 13mm diameter (item # NI0-1/2X1/8 (not shown on the diagram))

_One brass reducer (item # RE1/8FX1/4MS (not shown on the diagram))

From indexfasteners.com

_Two plug buttons (part O, item # SS48154K5900)

From amazon.com

_Twin socket adapter (part P)

From mcmaster.com

_Box of wire connectors (item # 7108K32 (not shown on the diagram))

_Length of white wire, 3048mm (item # 7587K138 (not shown on the diagram))

_Length of black wire, 3048mm (item # 7587K133 (not shown on the diagram))

_Electrical tape (item # 76455A21 (not shown on the diagram))

Tools

_Wire strippers

_Screwdriver

1

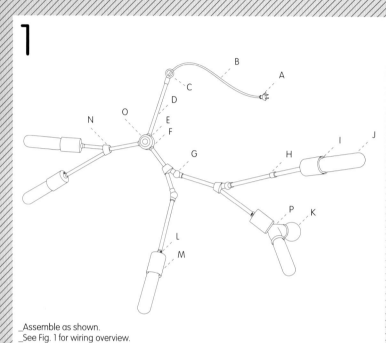

A
B
C
D
E
F
G
H
I
J
K
L
M
N
O
P

_Assemble as shown.
_See Fig. 1 for wiring overview.

2

D
L
Screw
M

White wire

Black wire

Top socket piece of Part I

Screw

Gold screw
Silver screw

Strip wire, twist around
screw and tighten

I

Screws inside socket

Wiring the socket cup
This is a generic wiring diagram, adapt
   to local specifications.
_Run one black and one white wire from each
   socket to the cluster body.
_Strip both wires.
_Attach the black wire to the gold screw and the
   white wire to the silver screw (see Fig. 2,3,4).

Fig. 1

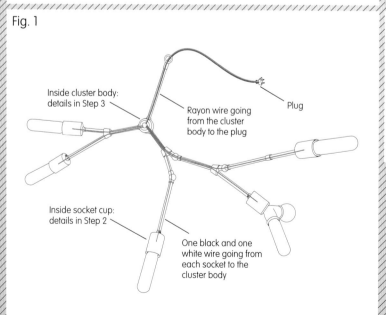

Inside cluster body:
details in Step 3

Rayon wire going
from the cluster
body to the plug

Plug

Inside socket cup:
details in Step 2

One black and one
white wire going from
each socket to the
cluster body

Fig. 2

Fig. 3

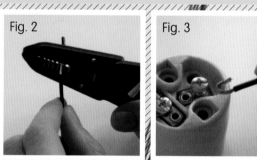

Fig. 4

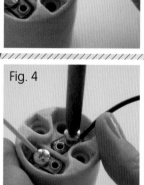

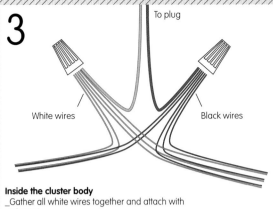

3

To plug

White wires

Black wires

Inside the cluster body
_Gather all white wires together and attach with wire nut.
_Gather all black wires together and attach with wire nut.

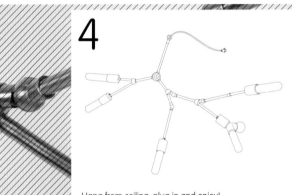

4

_Hang from ceiling, plug in and enjoy!

Get an electrician to help you hard-wire the light if you want to operate it from a switch.

QOOQOO LAMP

MOOMOO ARCHITECTS

Have you ever been taken by surprise not to see a light-bulb inside as expected when switching on a lamp. Such is the case with the Qooqoo Lamp designed by Polish architects MOOMOO. Several metres of corrugated pipe result in a design that gives a soft, romantic glow of light. But instead of a light source surrounded by shading, here the entire surface of the lamp provides the light, creating even, diffused lighting.

Making this lamp should be as fun as using it. MOOMOO insists that you experiment with the inner metal structure by trying different lengths of bar and bending at various points. Try making a taller floor version or a small desk lamp. Qooqoo can also be adapted by using different coloured LED ropelights.

You will need:

Materials

_Plastic corrugated pipe, 40mm diameter, 50m long

_LED ropelight, 2m long with power cord and switch

_Aluminium bar, 10mm diameter, 4–5m long

_Large and small cable ties

Tools

_Pliers to bend the aluminium

1

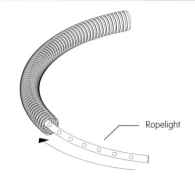

Ropelight

_If your LED ropelight did not come with a cord, wire in this order: plug, cable, switch, cable, LED ropelight.
_Place the LED ropelight inside the plastic pipe and wind the pipe into circles.

2

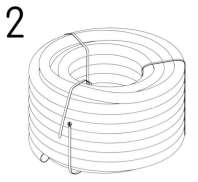

_Secure the coiled plastic pipe with large cable ties.

3

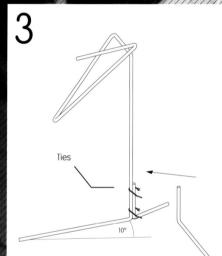

Ties

10°

_Bend the aluminium bar as shown (or as you like), creating one bend for a leg and several bends at the top to support the coil.
_Bend two shorter bars to make additional legs. You can paint these if you like.
_Attach the legs with small cable ties.

4

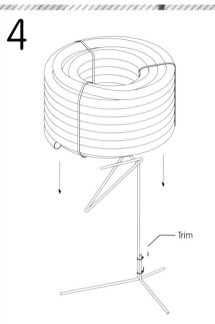

Trim

_Place the coiled plastic pipe over the metal base with the electrical cord on the inside positioned along the leg.

5

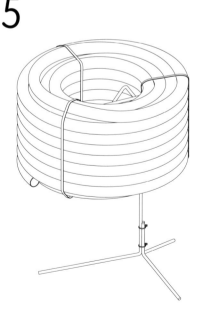

_Plug in and enjoy!

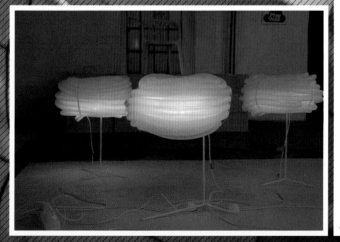

4.
SEATING

Many of us share a love of well-designed seating. Historically, four legs and a plank were good enough; more recently seating has formed some of the most iconic silhouettes in design history. So what makes a good modern seat? It has to rest our minds, our backs and our behinds. If that isn't enough, it has to do so with style.

Even in the most modest environments, available seats usually outnumber the number of people. After all, your guests need a place to sit so that they can admire all of your newly built furniture. This can get expensive, but fortunately this chapter includes some budget-friendly seating solutions. This is the money-and-resource-saving mentality of our contributors, like those at Recession Design who provide a hammock-inspired chair that moulds itself to the body by using a rubber floor mat as its main material. Their other project is a chair and stool that sandwich foam between simple, cut-out silhouettes.

But once again, it is the adaptation of ordinary materials that makes these pieces unique: sound insulation, shipping blankets, carpet padding, even flour-filled pond liner are here used to provide some cush for the tush.

POLTRONA (ARMCHAIR)

NICOLA GOLFARI FOR RECESSION DESIGN

This low-slung chair is formed from a rubber doormat hung hammock-like from a shaped chrome handrail with some cable ties. Hydraulic pipes are used for structure and some garden hose connectors are used as internal spacers. Complex yet simple at the same time, the result is a high-end design armchair that you can built in your garage on a Sunday.

Nicola writes: 'Too often "hand made" means "bad made". My personal purpose was to follow the "recession design philosophy" obtaining a design object that, at first sight, is not clearly identifiable as "hand made". For this reason I used metal tubes and rubber, materials normally used in industrial processes and products, finding how to assemble them in a very easy way. Only a closer view of the object reveals the simple objects used for the project like the handrail, cable zip ties and doormat.

'A final but important aspect in "DIY" philosophy is the possibility to customize the object: for this armchair, once you have built the metal structure, you can choose to change the hung material (to fabric carpet, metal net, etc.) to obtain different results.'

The design was exhibited in 2009 at MAK Vienna, the Austrian Museum of Applied Arts/Contemporary Art. The designer Nicola Golfari is Art Director of Recession Design (see also pages 32, 76, 92, 108 and 116).

You will need:

Materials

_Rubber doormat 500 x 1000mm (part A)

_Chrome handrail tube 40mm diameter, 4.2m long

_Hydraulic pipe, 9mm diameter, 4.2m long

_Eight 90-degree chromed handrail curves, 40mm diameter (part B)

_Eight 90-degree hydraulic pipe curves, 9mm diameter (part C)

_Nine hydraulic pipe couplings, 9mm diameter (part D)

_Length of metal pipe 250mm, with diameter that fits inside 9mm hydraulic pipe (part O)

_Four plastic water hose connectors

_Black plastic cable ties (part P)

_Metal glue

Tools

_Handsaw

_Pipe cutters

_Pipe wrench

1

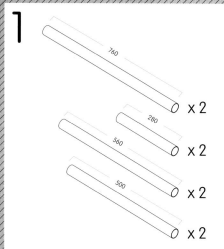

760 x 2
280 x 2
560 x 2
500 x 2

_Use the pipe cutters to cut the 40mm diameter chrome handrail to the following lengths:
_Two x 760mm (part E)
_Two x 280mm (part F)
_Two x 560mm (part G)
_Two x 500mm (part H).

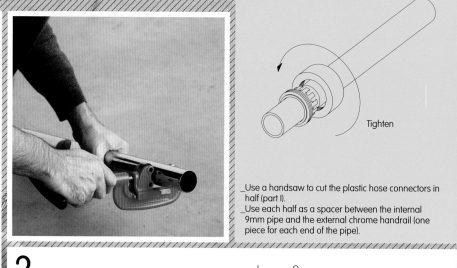

2

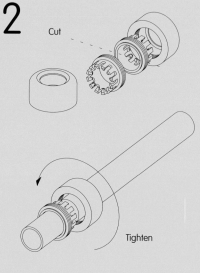

Cut

Tighten

_Use a handsaw to cut the plastic hose connectors in half (part I).
_Use each half as a spacer between the internal 9mm pipe and the external chrome handrail (one piece for each end of the pipe).

3

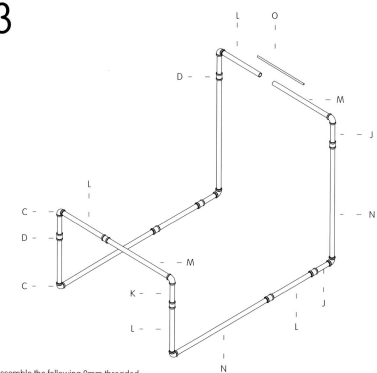

L   O

D

M

J

N

L

C

D

M

C

K

L

J

L

N

_Assemble the following 9mm threaded hydraulic pipe lengths as shown:
_Four x 60mm (part J)
_Two x 70mm (part K)
_Six x 200mm (part L)
_Two x 300mm (part M)
_Four x 500mm (part N).
_Save part O for Step 4.

4

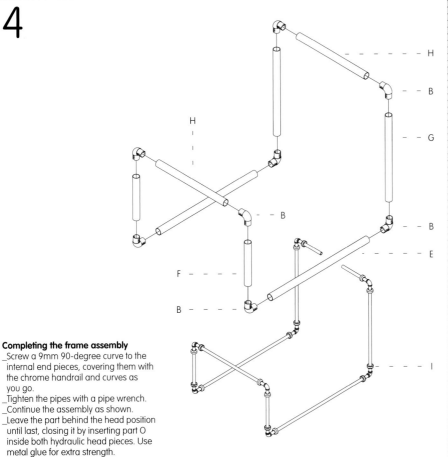

Completing the frame assembly

_Screw a 9mm 90-degree curve to the internal end pieces, covering them with the chrome handrail and curves as you go.
_Tighten the pipes with a pipe wrench.
_Continue the assembly as shown.
_Leave the part behind the head position until last, closing it by inserting part O inside both hydraulic head pieces. Use metal glue for extra strength.

5

_Use heavy-duty plastic cable ties to attach the rubber doormat (part A) to the upper and lower horizontal rails of the frame.

6

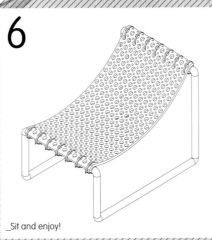

_Sit and enjoy!

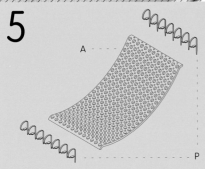

TO BECOME ONE SEAT

ERWIN ZWIERS

Inspiration for the 'Leave your shape behind' collection of which this seat is a part, comes from the beach. Sand is attractive to touch, to play with and to form shapes with. Here flour is substituted for sand, but in these rubber shapes it has the same attraction, making you want to touch it, play with it and make it into different shapes.

The To Become One Seat has two parts: the sack, which is formless, and the wooden frame construction. The sacks defy a definite form, just like sand on the beach. But by reinforcing each other the two parts become one.

The seats are designed to be sat on but also to be felt, kneaded and played with. With its soft, deformable bags this series offers a relaxing way of communicating. The interaction between the product and the user(s) makes it highly suitable for use when difficult issues are being discussed during brainstorming sessions and meetings, but also privately at home. In the middle of a conversation you can grab the seat and mould and deform it, which can have a relaxing effect.

In addition to their interesting appearance, the To Become One seats are surprisingly comfortable. When sat on the sacks adapt ergonomically to the shape of the body.

You will need:

Materials

_Wooden dowel, 28mm diameter, 6300m long

_18 L bolts M6 (6mm) x 35mm L bolts, 18 M6 nuts

_36 flat washers (metal spacers) with 6mm hole and 14mm outside diameter

_Two sheets of rubber pond liner, 700 x 700mm

_Flour, 10kg

_Wood glue

Tools

_Saw

_Tightening spanner

_Pen

_Sewing machine (optional) or needle and thread for sewing pond liner

_Heavy-duty scissors (to cut pond liner)

_Plug cutter, 14mm

_Mallet

_Drill

_Drill bit, 6mm

_Flat spade bit, 14mm

_Funnel (you can make one with a bucket and pipe, see page 75)

1

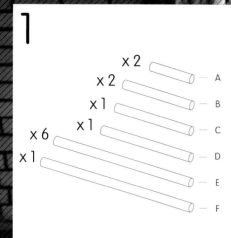

x 2 — A
x 2 — B
x 1 — C
x 1 — D
x 6 — E
x 1 — F

_Using the saw, cut the wooden dowel to the
following lengths:
_Two x 150mm (part A)
_Two x 250mm (part B)
_One x 275mm (part C)
_One x 325mm (part D)
_Six x 500mm (part E)
_One x 550mm, (part F).

2

x 2

A   30°   30°   B

150
x 2
Tighten

350
Tighten
E
E   550

_Make an x shape using two part E's, crossing them
at about 350mm from the bottom.
_Drill through both dowels with a 6mm bit, then drill
17mm deep on one side of each dowel with a 14mm
flat spade bit (see Fig. 1)
_Place a metal washer (part H) in each hole and join
the dowels with M6 bolt (part G) and nut (part I).
_Join one part A with one part B, adjusting to about 30
degrees to make a cross piece.
_Repeat so that you have two of each piece.

Fig. 1

Drill

28

G
H
H
I

17

6
14

3

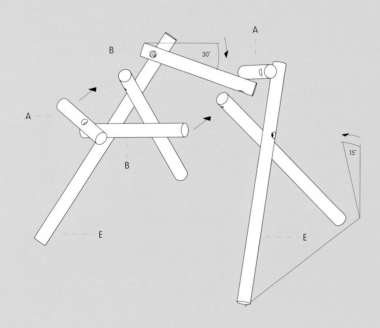

A
B
30°
A
B
E
15°
E

_Assemble all four pieces as shown.
_Lean the x shapes in about 15 degrees.
_Connect the two x shapes by attaching an A/B cross
piece, slightly rotating the middle down by 30 degrees
(you will end up with a part A (shorter dowel) on one
side and a part B on the other).
_Now connect the second A/B cross piece; this time the
shorter part (A) will be on the opposite side.

4

E   D   E

_Connect part D to the two cross pieces (parts A and B)
by joining across the top or underside.
_Stabilize the bottom of each x with another part E about
60–100mm from the floor. It's fine to make it crooked!

5

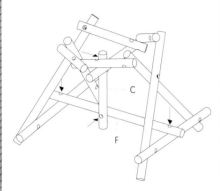

C

F

_Attach a long cross piece (part F) to the two stabilizing pieces from Step 4.
_Attach a vertical bar (part C) to part D and part F.
_Tighten all the nuts and bolts.

6

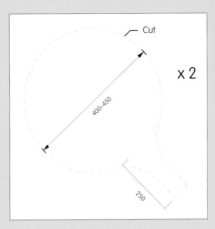

Cut

400–450

250

x 2

_Draw a circle on the pond liner about 400–450mm in diameter with a 250mm length added to make a balloon shape.
_Cut the shape out with the scissors.
_Repeat, so that you have two balloon shapes.

7

Fill

Sew

_Sew the two balloon shapes together.
_Fill with flour.
_Tie a knot in the end.

8

_Take a scrap of the dowel and using a 14mm plug cutter cut 64 wooden plugs.
_Hide the nuts and bolts by pushing wooden plugs into the holes. Add a little wood glue to the hole first and tap in gently with a rubber mallet.
_Lay the seat over the frame and relax.

SEDIA E SGABELLO

LUCA BUTTAFAVA AND ALESSANDRO CONFALONIERI
FOR RECESSION DESIGN

The chair S.1 and stool Sg.1 designed by the INTERSEZIONI
Design Studio of Alessandro Confalonieri and Luca Buttafava
are constructed with layers of plywood and polystyrene foam
assembled with threaded rods. In this sandwich construction the
layer of foam serves as a cushion and reduces the overall weight
of the chair.

With this piece the designers wanted to stress the construction
method as much as possible, and have designed something
that is more than just an ordinary piece of DIY. Within the area
of DIY there are people who are capable of constructing very
sophisticated and articulated objects. For many it is a real 'way of
life'. Although this piece is relatively simple to construct,
its design is truly original.

A natural evolution of this 'open source' experiment is a low-cost
variation that uses cardboard instead of plywood, and there are
no limits to the material that could be used and how the design
could be interpreted.

You will need:

Materials

_Two sheets of plywood, 22 x 1524
x 1524mm

_Sheet of polystyrene foam, 20 x 2400
x 1200mm

_Threaded stainless steel rod, 8mm
diameter, 2.512m long

_26 stainless steel M8 (female
portion) furniture connecting screws
with allen head and sleeve nut to
screw onto the threaded rod

Tools

_Circular saw

_Jigsaw

_Hacksaw (for the threaded rods)

_Long blade or light bandsaw

_Drill

_Allen key

1

Part A

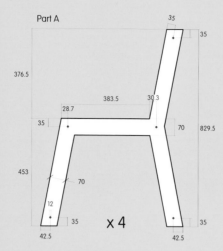

35
35
376.5
383.5
30.3
28.7
35
70
829.5
453
70
12
35
42.5
42.5
35

x 4

Part B

12
376.5
384
11.25°
455
11.25°
28.7
70
35
35
12
455
27.1

x 6

Part C

470
28.7
28.7
35
70
70
369
11.25°
12
35
35
42.5
59.5
355
59.5
42.5

x 4

Part D

470
28.7
28.7
35
70
498
12

x 6

_Use a circular saw to make wood silhouettes from the plywood following the dimensions above.
_Finish all the angles with a jigsaw to make the following:
Four x side silhouettes for chair (part A)
Six x inner silhouettes for chair (part B)
Four x side silhouettes for stool (part C)
Six x inner silhouettes for stool (part D).
_Drill 12 mm holes where marked (the hole size is determined by the outer dimension of the connecting screw).
_Finish with sandpaper.

2

Cutting the foam

Part E
(same as B, just add 15mm)

35
12
8.5
70
35
42.6
27.1

x 9

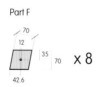

Part F

70
12
35
70

x 8

42.6

Part G
(same as D, just add 15mm)

35
70
85
12
42.6

x 9

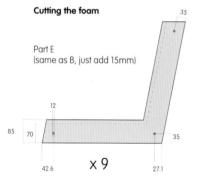

_Use the long blade or light bandsaw to make the following silhouettes from the foam polystyrene:
_Nine x inner foam upper silhouettes for chair (part E)
_Eight x inner foam lower silhouettes for chair and stool (part F)
_Nine x inner foam upper silhouettes for stool (part G).
_Drill 12 mm holes where marked.

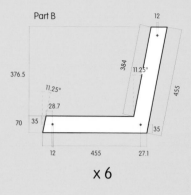

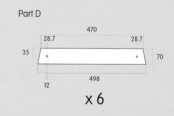

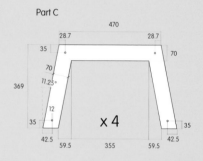

3

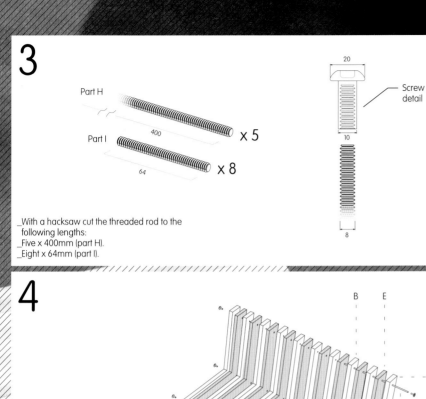

Part H

400

x 5

Part I

64

x 8

20

Screw detail

10

8

_With a hacksaw cut the threaded rod to the
following lengths:
_Five x 400mm (part H).
_Eight x 64mm (part I).

4

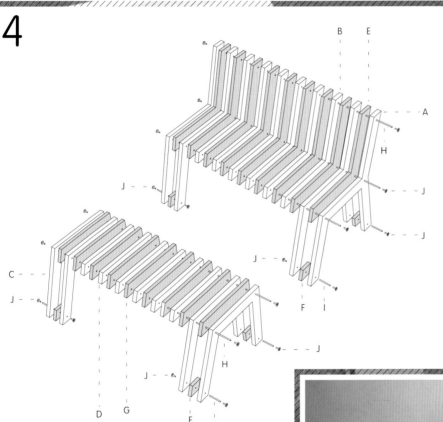

B   E

A

H

J

J

J

F   I

C

J

F   I

J

H

J

D   G

F   I

_Assemble both chair and stool by placing the long
threaded rods into one side silhouette and then stacking
each piece as shown.
_Once all the pieces are together, cut the rod flush
with the side silhouette (be careful not to damage
the threads).
_Tighten the pieces together with the connecting screws
(part J).

5

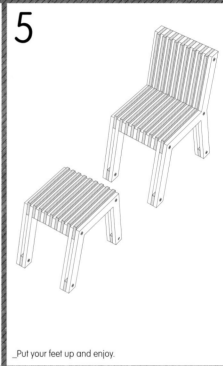

_Put your feet up and enjoy.

HOPELESS DIAMOND SOFA

CHRISTOPHER STUART OF LUUR STUDIO

This sofa was inspired by a folding paper cup that the author was taught to make as a child, which tapered towards the base and revealed triangular shapes from the folding process on the inside. Here the box perimeter has been retained and the trapezoids and triangles taper, creating a multi-faceted form similar to that seen on the F-117 stealth aircraft – 'Hopeless Diamond' was an early nickname given to the aircraft.

The focus of this prototype version was to use off-the-shelf materials found at the local DIY store like copper plumbing pipe (for the base frame of the sofa), shipping blankets, cable ties and carpet padding. The design can be adapted by choosing your favourite wood and different coloured cable ties or fabric.

You will need:

Materials

_Sheet of wood 19 x 1220 x 2440mm. Here it is solid walnut, but cabinet-grade plywood is fine too.

_44 medium cable ties

_2.14m length of 25mm-wide nylon straps (here two 1828mm straps from a ratchet strap)

_Six 3m lengths of copper pipe type L (it is stronger), 19mm diameter

_26 copper Ts (part T)

_12 90-degree copper elbows (part U)

_Two rolls of 19mm self-stick Velcro

_Two shipping blankets 1829 x 2032 mm

_Sheet of foam or carpet padding 25 x 1220 x 2440mm. Use 38mm thick foam if you want more cushion.

Tools

_Pipe cutter

_Pipe brush

_Flux

_Solder

_Propane torch

_Router with 6mm bevel bit

_Sewing machine

_Scissors

_Drill

_Drill bit, 6mm

1

_Cut the copper pipe to the following lengths:

Rectangle
_Two x 884mm (part A)
_Two x 156mm (part B)
_Two x 706mm (part C)
_Two x 230mm (part D)
_Two x 630mm (part E).

Back
_Three x 244mm (part F)
_Two x 154mm (part G)
_Two x 705mm (part H)
_Six x 51mm (part I)
_Two x 479mm (part J).

Seat
_Two x 548mm (part K)
_Three x 108mm (part L)
_Two x 176mm (part M)
_Two x 51mm (part I)
_One x 338mm (part N).

Legs
_Two x 51mm (part I)
_Two x 481mm (part O)
_Two x 629mm (part P)
_Two x 125mm (part Q)
_Three x 216mm (part R)
_Three x 198mm (part S).

2

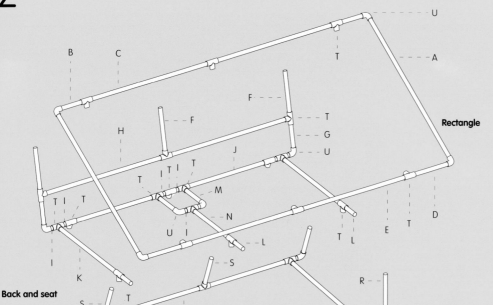

Rectangle

Back and seat

Legs

like so!

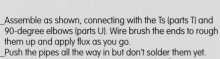

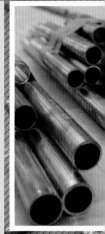

_Assemble as shown, connecting with the Ts (parts T) and
 90-degree elbows (parts U). Wire brush the ends to rough
 them up and apply flux as you go.
_Push the pipes all the way in but don't solder them yet.
_Assemble the rectangle as one unit and lay flat.
_Assemble the back and seat together and attach to the
 rectangle. It is easier to have the frame upside down for this.
_Attach the legs and carefully turn the frame right side up.
_Check that the rectangle is square by measuring corner to
 corner and checking that the opposite corner measurement
 is the same.
_Check that the pipes are parallel by measuring the space
 between pipes at each end.

3

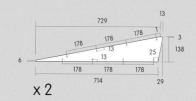
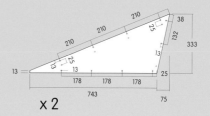
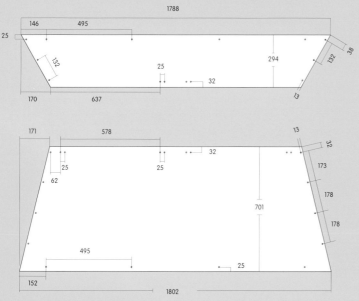

x 2

x 2

_Using the saw cut the 19mm thick wood into
the six pieces shown above. Note that you will need
two of each triangle.
_Drill 6mm holes along the edges as shown.

4

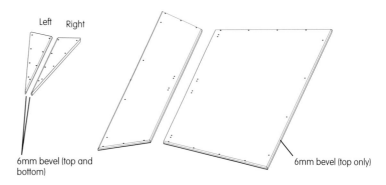

Left   Right

6mm bevel (top and
bottom)

6mm bevel (top only)

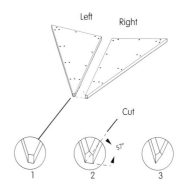

Left   Right

Cut

57°

1   2   3

_Use a router to cut a 6mm bevel to the edges
shown here in red.
_For the large trapezoid, bevel the long edge and
the sides (not the short edge) of the side that you
want to be facing out.
_For the small trapezoid, bevel all four edges of
the side you want to be facing out.
_For the small triangles, you will have a left and a
right. Bevel the 714mm edges on both sides.
_For the large triangles, you will also have a left
and right. Bevel all three edges of the side you
want to be facing out.
_From the outside bottom corner of the 13mm end,
cut a 57-degree mitre the entire length of the
743mm edge.

5

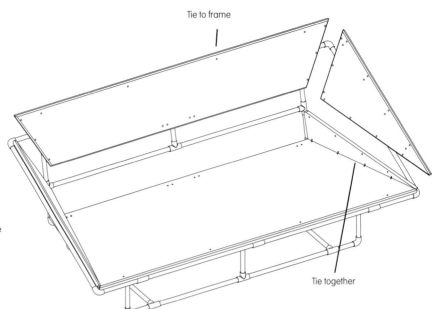

Tie to frame

Tie together

_Test the fit of the boards to the frame, pushing
and pulling on the copper to make a good fit.
_Remove boards and solder the pipe. Hold
the torch at the middle of the elbow or T. When the
T is hot enough, the heat will draw the solder into
the fitting for a strong hold.
_Before tying the boards down, trace their shape
onto the shipping blankets, adding 25mm all the
way around.
_Repeat on the foam, but subtract 25mm all the
way around.
_Where two board edges touch, use a cable tie to join
together with the cable head to the back.
_Everywhere else tie the boards to the frame.

6

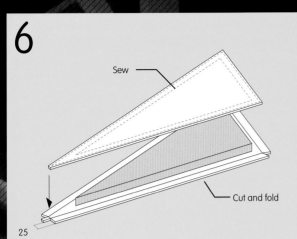

Sew

Cut and fold

25

_From the shipping blankets, cut two parts for each cushion.
_The extra 25mm forms an edge seam. Notch the corners, fold in and sew two lines 6mm and 19mm from the edge on all sides.
_Cut the foam out and seal it between the two blanket shapes, sewing or using self-stick Velcro to close.
_Repeat for all cushions.

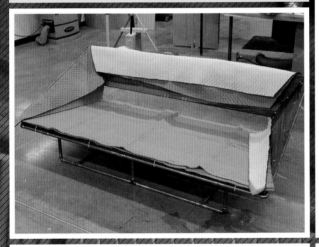

7

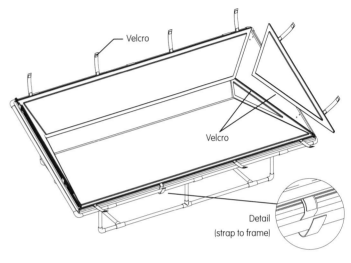

Velcro

Velcro

Detail
(strap to frame)

_Cut the 25mm wide nylon strap into 12 lengths of 178mm. Sew 25mm of the strap into the cushion edges that form the perimeter of the rectangle.
_Attach four straps along the top edge of the top cushion, four along the front edge of the seat and two along each top edge of the large triangle.
_Use a lighter to melt the nylon edges (to keep them from fraying) and sew on a 25 x 25mm square of Velcro.
_Strap the fabric to the frame by going under the wood, behind the pipe and back up, securing with Velcro.

8

_Sit back, pull your feet up and enjoy.

THE PANTHER

MAX SANJULIAN OF VOLIDO

This project gets its name from the poem 'The Panther' by Rainer Maria Rilke. The poem describes a panther trapped by the bars that cage him, catching glances of the outside world as he turns circles inside what has become a comfortable shelter. The wild panther seems tame until his glance is interrupted by something that has caught his eye through the bars.

This may be the imagery that has inspired the designer. The Panther sofa's box form provides a secluded shelter, padded and enhanced by the repeated pyramidal shapes of the sound dampening foam. Or the sofa itself may be the interesting thing that has caught the panther's eye.

Although the sofa is said to be comfortable, comfort is not the first priority for the designer. 'In design I'm not very interested in aspects of being comfortable or ergonomic, and what the function of a piece of furniture is or if furniture has to have a function at all. Nowadays, this could be a long discussion. High heels are not comfortable. Dildos and brassieres are not exactly comfortable either, and their function or their ergonomic aspects are more than dubious. On the other hand, they are able to express or carry with them other human conditions. These conditions may be more important than being comfortable. Surprisingly at the end, this design is very comfortable and the ergonomics look good.'

You will need:

Materials

_Sheet of cabinet-grade plywood 19 x 1500 x 3000mm

_Eight tiles of 102 x 610 x 610mm pyramid sound foam

_Three timber struts 51 x 51 x 2400mm

_39 screws (28 x 45mm screws for the plywood to plywood or plywood to timbers, 11 x 75mm screws for the timbers)

_Glue for foam and for wood

Tools

_Drill

_Plug cutter

_Saw

_Clamps

1

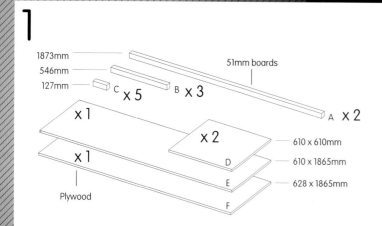

1873mm
546mm
127mm

C x 5   B x 3   51mm boards

x 1   x 2   A x 2

x 1   D   610 x 610mm
E   610 x 1865mm
F   628 x 1865mm

Plywood

_Cut the 51 x 51mm timber to the following lengths:
_Two x 1873mm (part A)
_Three x 546mm (part B)
_Five x 127mm (part C).
_Cut the 19mm plywood to the following sizes:
_Two x 610 x 610mm (part D)
_One x 610 x 1865mm (part E)
_One x 628 x 1865mm (part F).

2

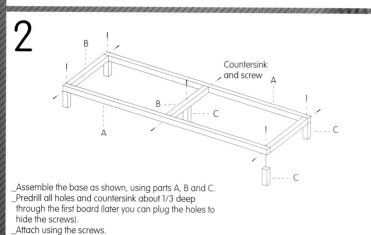

B
Countersink
and screw   A
B   C
A   C
C

_Assemble the base as shown, using parts A, B and C.
_Predrill all holes and countersink about 1/3 deep
  through the first board (later you can plug the holes to
  hide the screws).
_Attach using the screws.

3

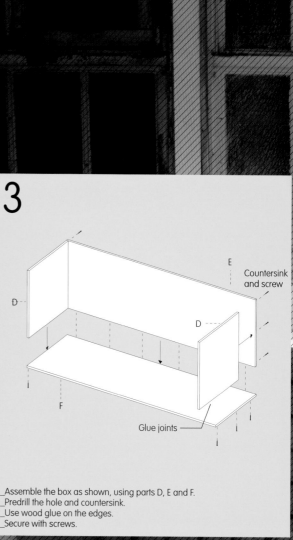

E
Countersink
and screw
D
D
F
Glue joints

_Assemble the box as shown, using parts D, E and F.
_Predrill the hole and countersink.
_Use wood glue on the edges.
_Secure with screws.

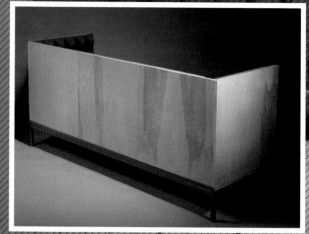

4

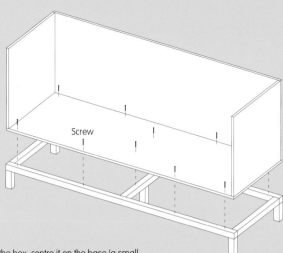

Screw

_To attach the box, centre it on the base (a small
ledge of the base will be visible all the way around).
_Clamp and predrill the holes.
_Remove the box, and apply glue where the base
meets the plywood.
_Secure with screws. These will not be plugged, but
the screws do need to be flush with the surface so
that they don't stick through the foam later.

5

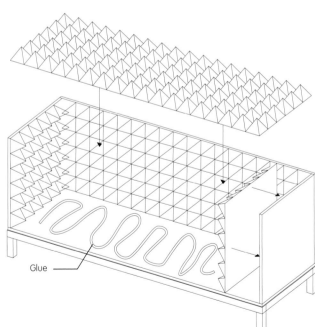

Glue

_To attach the pyramid sound foam cut the foam to the
interior dimensions of the box.
_Check the fit by laying the foam in the box.
_Stick the foam to the plywood with some glue for foam.

6

_Sit back and enjoy.

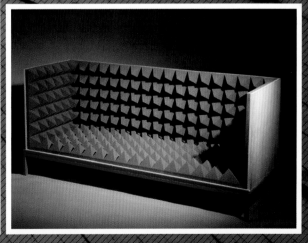

5.
BEDROOM

Prepare to preen! It's easy to have an organized day when you start out that way. Your favourite outfits and shoes await behind the upcycled closed doors of the Oddstock Floored Wardrobe which is elegantly patterned in hardwood flooring.

Don't forget your hair and make-up! Brooklyn design group, Uhuru, also upcycled by turning a common saw horse into the base for their industrial, but feminine vanity, aptly titled Warehouse Vanity.

When you are ready to retire after a long day, sit back in the Italian-designed Divano Letto Sofabed or extend its side with a simple slide and you're really ready to take a load off your feet. Set the alarm for relax and take a snooze. Tomorrow is a new day.

DIVANO LETTO SOFABED

MARISSA MORELLI FOR RECESSION DESIGN

Unlike most sofabeds that extend outwards from the front, this single sofabed extends from the sides. During the day it's a comfortable sofa, at night you just slide the lower part towards the outside and it becomes a bed. The structure is made up of timber slats and boards and is simple to construct, using nails and screws. The cushions and mattress are made of foam covered with grey industrial felt and sewn by hand.

Inspiration came from the designer's need to have a small sofa in her small house, which could then double up as a bed for guests. The lines of the piece are inspired by Dutch furniture design of the 1930s. The sofabed was exhibited in 2009 at MAK Vienna, the Austrian Museum of Applied Arts/Contemporary Art.

You will need:

Materials

_Two sheets of plywood 30 x 1220mm x 1220mm

_Eleven wood boards 35 x 70 x 1400mm

_Sheet of foam rubber 90 x 500 x 700mm

_Sheet of foam rubber 50 x 700 x 1400mm

_Roll of felt large enough to cover foam

_Screws 35mm and 50mm long

_Orange cotton yarn and a large needle

_Wood glue

_Paint (optional)

Tools

_Screwdriver

_Scissors

_Saw

_Drill

_Countersink bit

_Sandpaper

_Plug cutter

1

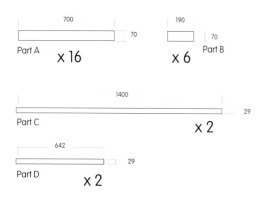

Part A x 16
700 x 70

Part B x 6
190 x 70

Part C x 2
1400 x 29

Part D x 2
642 x 29

_For the frame cut the boards to the following sizes:
_Sixteen x 700 x 70mm (part A – slats)
_Six x 190 x 70mm (part B – feet)
_Two x 1400 x 29mm (part C – sides of frame)
_Two x 642 x 29mm (part D – ends of frame).

2

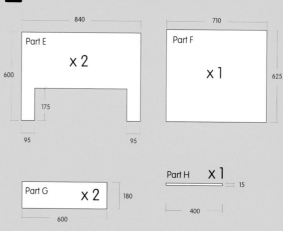

Part E x 2
840 x 600, 175, 95, 95

Part F x 1
710 x 625

Part G x 2
600 x 180

Part H x 1
400 x 15

_For the bed ends and sliding board cut the plywood to
  the following sizes:
_Two x 840 x 600mm, cut the section out of the bottom
  as shown (part E)
_One x 710 x 625mm (part F)
_Two x 600 x 180mm (part G).
_One x 400 x 15mm (part H).

3

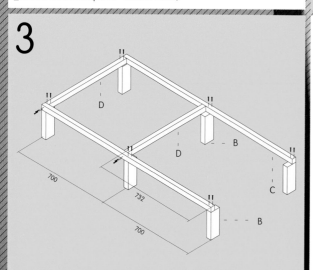

_Assemble the frame as shown.
_Drill pilot holes with a countersink bit about 1/3 through
  the first board and use long screws to secure together.
_The centre brace (part D) is offset for the slider board to
  rest on.

4

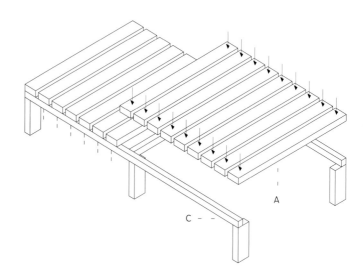

_Attach the slats (parts A) by placing on the frame (parts
  C) and screwing in from underneath through parts C.
_With a plug cutter the size of the countersink bit
  create wood plugs to plug the holes and hide the
  screws. Use a little glue on the plug and sand
  smooth when the glue dries.
_If you want to paint the frame, do so at this stage. On
  the example shown here only the frame is painted.

5

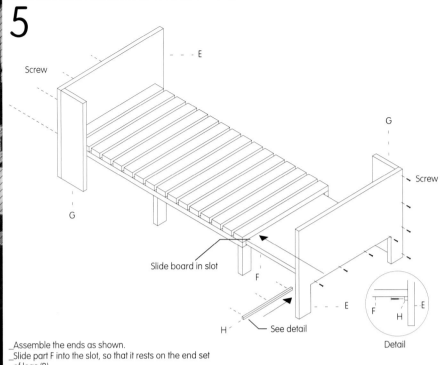

Screw
— E
G

G

Screw

Slide board in slot

F

See detail

E

H

Detail

F E
H

_Assemble the ends as shown.
_Slide part F into the slot, so that it rests on the end set
 of legs (B).
_Countersink and screw part E to part G. Repeat to make
 the other end.
_Attach one end to part F by countersinking and screwing
 through part E.
_Attach the scrap board (part H) to part E from the inside,
 creating a ledge to support part F.
_Screw the other end to the frame.
_Fill the holes with wood plugs and sand smooth.

6

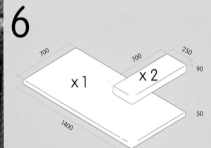

700
700
250
90
x 1
x 2
1400
50

_Cut the foam to the following sizes:
_One x 50 x 700 x 1400mm
_Two x 90 x 250 x 700mm
_Cut the felt to cover the foam, sew it together with the
 orange thread.

7

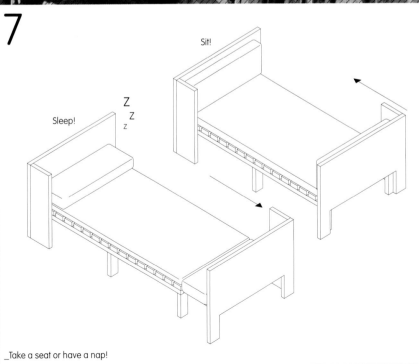

Sit!

Z
Z
z

Sleep!

_Take a seat or have a nap!

WAREHOUSE VANITY

UHURU DESIGN

Many of the pieces created by the design group Uhuru utilize repurposed materials. For the Warehouse Vanity they used an office pencil drawer, a sawhorse and several exposed light-bulbs. They wanted to combine feminine beauty with an industrial masculine feel. The light-bulbs are a reference to the classic dressing room vanity, while the sawhorse gives the vanity a new identity. The drawer allows for storage, while the pivoting mirrors on the sides help with visibility.

Uhuru wanted to create a piece that would be functional and easy to make. Sawhorses come in many sizes. Once you have found a sawhorse, you can adjust the vanity top to the dimensions. Alternately, you can mount LED light strips to the top instead. Some are small enough that you can just use double-sided tape to stick them to the panel. There are usually several options to choose from.

You will need:

Materials

_Four standard light kits with sockets and at least 2m of cord

_Sheet of plywood or fibreboard 13 x 1220 x 1220mm

_Roll of adhesive felt 13mm wide (part I)

_Three mirror tiles 305 x 305mm (parts J)

_Two piano hinges, 254mm long

_Pencil drawer. If not available make one from the parts F, G and H in Step 1

_Metal sawhorse with handle, height adjusted to 620mm, other dimensions 430 x 915mm

_40 screws, 12 to 19mm long

_Two top-mounting drawer slides, roughly 380mm long when in closed position

_Paint (optional), one colour for the sawhorse and one for the top and drawer

_Glue for mirror tiles

Tools

_Saw

_Screwdriver

_Pencil

1

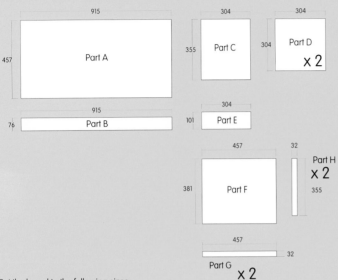

915
Part A
457

915
Part B
76

304
Part C
355

304
Part D
× 2
304
304

304
Part E
101

457
Part F
381

32
Part H
× 2
355

457
Part G
× 2
32

_Cut the board to the following sizes:
_One x 915 x 457mm (part A)
_One x 915 x 76mm (part B)
_One x 304 x 355mm (part C)
_Two x 304 x 304mm (part D)
_One x 304 x 101mm (part E).

_For the drawer (not needed if reusing
an existing drawer):
_One x 457 x 381mm (part F)
_Two x 457 x 32mm (part G)
_Two x 355 x 32mm (part H).

2

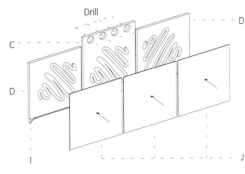

Drill

C
D
D
I
J

Preparing the plywood
_Paint both sides of the plywood (optional).
_Apply felt (part I) to the bottom of the two side pieces (parts D).
This will stop them from scratching the surface of the vanity.
_Glue the mirrors (parts J) to the three panels (parts C and D). The
two side panels should have the mirror flush with the bottom,
while the middle panel should have the mirror 3mm from the
bottom to account for the felt on the bottom of the side panels.
_Leave to dry for 24 hours.
_When the mirrors are dry, drill holes for the four light fixtures in
the top 500mm of the centre panel. We used a standard size
bulb, so the hole had a 38mm diameter. Measure your lights
first and adjust the size of the hole to fit.
_To get a snug fit, apply a strip of adhesive felt to the inside of
the hole. Be sure that the strip is no bigger than 12mm so that it
doesn't stick out.

3

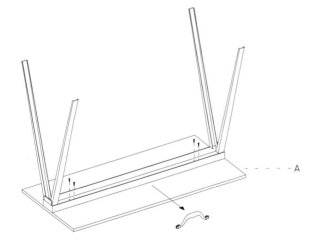

A

Preparing the base
_Remove the handle from the sawhorse by drilling the rivets out.
You can use a 3mm drill bit and trim the extra. This will become
the handle to the drawer face in Step 4.
_Adjust the sawhorse to the desired height, and if you want, paint
both the sawhorse and the handle.
_Centre the vanity top (part A) on the sawhorse and screw through
the bottom.

4

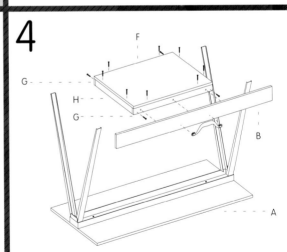

F
G
H
G
B
A

Assembling the drawer
_Uhuru recycled a pencil drawer, but you can make one
by using parts F, G and H. Follow the assembly above.
_Screw the drawer face (part B) to the pencil drawer from
inside. Screw the reused handle from the sawhorse to
the drawer face.

5

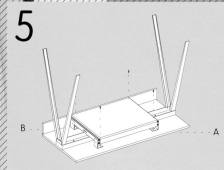

Attaching the drawer
_Mount the drawer to the bottom of the vanity top. Allow space for the drawer to slide beneath the sawhorse top.

6

Attaching the mirror section
_Centre the middle bracing (part E) so that it is flush with the back of the vanity top. Secure with screws from below.
_Secure the middle mirror panel (part C) in the same way by screwing from below.
_Mount the hinges between the centre panel and the sides. The mirrors should line up. Secure the side panels to the hinges.
_Slide the lights in through the back, and screw the light-bulbs in at the front.

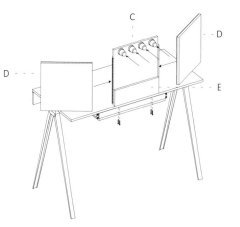

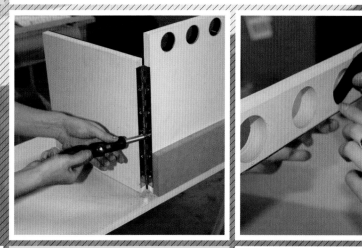

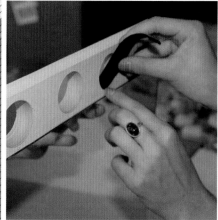

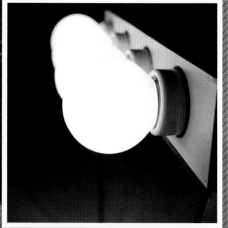

7

_Plug in, pull up a stool and preen.

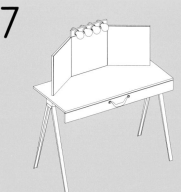

ODDSTOCK FLOORED WARDROBE

CHRISTOPHER STUART OF LUUR STUDIO

For any DIY enthusiast, the clearance bin at the DIY store is a regular stop. The Oddstock Floored Wardrobe was designed and built to take advantage of that bin. Brazilian teak prefinished hardwood flooring was found on clearance for an irresistible price. The box had apparently been returned from a large flooring job.

To make use of all the boards, they were cut to short, mitred pieces and arranged in a chevron pattern. Metal tile flooring dividers were used to hide the board edges, trimming out the doors. A simple box deep enough to house clothes on hangers was placed on Queen Anne legs for a romantic look. After many searches for the right door handles, utilitarian garage door handles were chosen because of their large size and casual appearance. A coat hook and mirror were added to the inside of the door for accessories.

You can change the look to be more modern by using straight legs instead. Fill the bottom with shoes or boxes and add shelves if you like, or try other types of wood flooring and experiment with different patterns.

You will need:

Materials

_Two sheets of plywood 19 x 1220 x 2440mm. Here cabinet-grade birch is used

_Sheet of plywood 6 x 1220 x 2440mm. Here cabinet-grade birch is used

_Sheet of MDF 13 x 1220 x 2440mm

_Box of tongue-and-groove hardwood flooring (here Brazilian teak), 9 x 76 x at least 254mm

_Metal clothes rail, 33mm diameter, at least 978mm long (part L)

_Set of brass clothes rail holders, 33mm diameter (part M)

_Four wooden Queen Anne style legs (part I), length 710mm

_Four metal tile flooring dividers, 9mm profile x 1.5mm metal thickness x 1903mm long (part J) (the profile hides the flooring edges. Match the profile height to your flooring thickness)

_Two brass utility door handles, 165mm long (part O)

_Four pairs of brass ball catches (part N)

_Screws 13–32mm long

_Small nails

_Four corner plates and mounting hardware for table legs (part K)

_Two brass piano hinges, 38mm wide when open, 1829mm long (part P)

_Wood glue and gel super glue with activator

Tools

_Screwdriver

_Drill

_Hacksaw

_Hammer

_Small nail gun or headless pin nailer

_Countersink bit

_Plug cutter

1

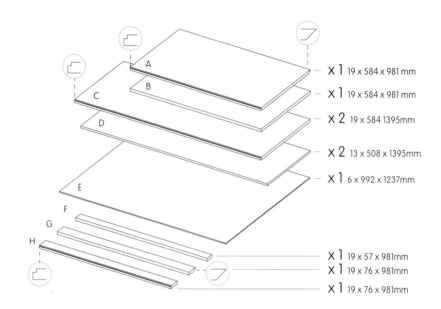

X 1 19 x 584 x 981 mm

X 1 19 x 584 x 981 mm

X 2 19 x 584 1395mm

X 2 13 x 508 x 1395mm

X 1 6 x 992 x 1237mm

X 1 19 x 57 x 981mm

X 1 19 x 76 x 981mm

X 1 19 x 76 x 981mm

_Cut the 19mm thick plywood to the following sizes:
 _One 584 x 981mm, mitre one long edge 45 degrees
 with a saw and notch a 6 x 6mm groove with a saw
 or router (part A)
 _One 584 x 981mm, unmitred (part B)
 _Two 584 x 1395mm, notch a 6 x 6mm groove with
 a saw or router (part C)
 _One 57 x 981mm (part F)
 _One 76 x 981mm, mitre one long edge 45 degrees
 with a saw (part G)
 _One 76 x 981mm, notch a 6 x 6mm groove with a
 saw or router (part H).
_Cut the 13mm thick MDF to the following sizes:
 Two 508 x 1395mm (part D)
_Cut the 6mm thick plywood to the following size:
 One 992 x 1235mm (part E)

2

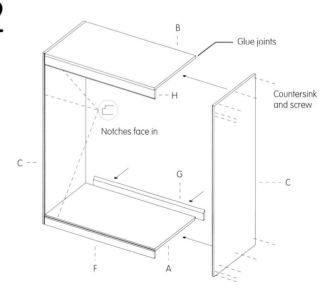

Glue joints

Countersink
and screw

Notches face in

_To assemble the box add wood glue to each joint.
_Smooth the glue with a credit card.
_Predrill holes with a countersink bit and screw together
 as needed. Sink the screws so that you can add wood
 plugs later.

3

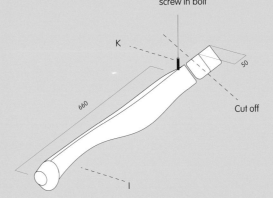

Drill hole and
screw in bolt

K

660

50

Cut off

I

_Cut each leg to 660mm.
_Drill and screw in the threaded rod from the corner
plate kit (part K) 28mm from the top.

4

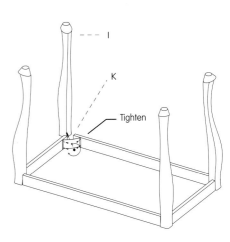

I

K

Tighten

Assembling the legs

_This is a two-part step:
_First, turn the box face down (not shown here) and place
a leg in each corner.
_Measure the spaces between the legs and cut scrap
pieces of plywood 19 x 57mm x the length of each gap.
_Now place the legs (parts I) and boards upside down
(as shown above) and assemble with the corner plate
kits (parts K).

5

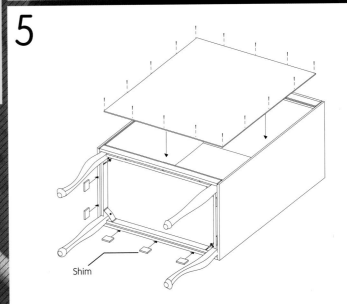

Shim

_Attach the leg assembly by screwing from the inside of
the box through the base of the box (part A).
_Using scrap plywood, cut wedges to fit between the box
and leg assembly (a tight fit will reduce wobble).
_Secure wedges with nails or screws.
_Attach the 6mm backer board (part E) with small nails.
Be careful with the angle of the nails, you don't want the
nail to show on the inside of the box.
_Use a plug cutter to make wood plugs. Fill the screw
holes with wood plugs using a little wood glue. Sand
smooth once the glue is dry.
_If you want to paint the structure, now is a good time to
do it. Don't forget the doors!

6

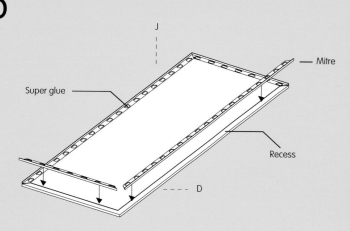

J

Mitre

Super glue

Recess

D

_Cut the metal tile dividers to the length and width of the door. Mitre the corners (part D).
_Use a router or electric planer to recess an area for the trim pieces (so that the flooring can sit flat).
_Use gel super glue to hold the trim in place by running a small bead of glue along the open areas (see Fig.1)

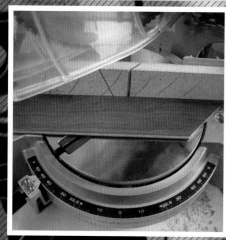

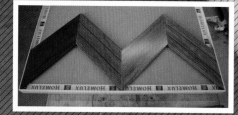

7

To edge of face (not tongue)

254

x 56

76

x 56

178

45

Left

Right

Cutting the flooring to size
_Cut each piece of flooring to 254mm with a 45-degree mitre on each side parallel to one another (do not include the tongue in the measurement). Depending on the direction the blade spins, one side will tear out. Turn your board over so that the tear is on the back.
_Start by cutting four 'lefts'. Flip two over to use as 'rights' so you can test the spacing (see Fig.2)
_Once your spacing looks good, cut 56 lefts and 56 rights.

8

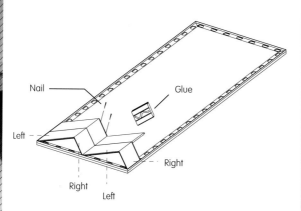

Nail

Glue

Left

Right

Right

Left

_Dry fit all of the pieces and cut the tongue off the filler pieces.
_Apply a bead of glue on the back of the board and attach by putting two nails in the tongue. Make sure you angle the nail gun.

9

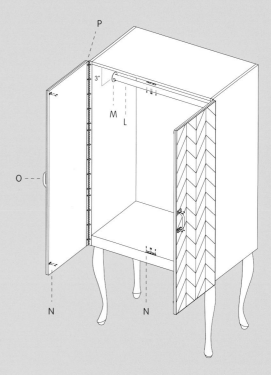

_Cut the piano hinges (parts P) to 1395mm with a hacksaw and attach the doors.

_Attach the brass door pulls (parts O) with screws long enough to partially go through the MDF (be sure to drill pilot holes first, so that you don't crack the hardwood flooring).

_Attach ball catches (parts N) with screws. Have one door open and mark the position of the catch on the closed door from the inside.

_ Cut the clothes rail (part L) to 978mm long and paint if you like. Mount it 76mm from the top to the centre of the bar, using the clothes rail hangers (parts M).

_Since this piece is tall, you should mount it to the wall by screwing through part H from the inside. You may need a spacer between part H and the wall.

10

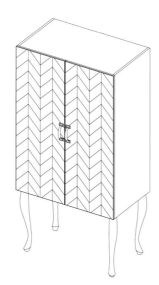

_Hang up your clothes and enjoy!

6. OUTDOOR

Home doesn't begin and end at the doorstep. Sometimes we need a break from the shelter of indoor living. The following designs will inspire you to take a breath of fresh air. Walk off a restless mind with Cristiano Urban's mobile Sunbed in tow and set it up in your favourite outdoor spot. A 'cushioned' chair cast in concrete will hold up to Mother Nature and put a smile on your face while you recharge your vitamin D. To set up camp anywhere, all you need is Fire Up, a DIY campfire kit designed to burn perfectly every time.

You don't necessarily have to be outside to feel outside. Green Screen creates the feeling of an outdoor environment in the comfort of your home or office. Turn any space into a pergola-inspired sanctuary and enjoy the plants while you make more furniture!

JESOLO SUNBED

CRISTIANO URBAN FOR RECESSION DESIGN

The design for the Jesolo Sunbed was the designer's response to the basic concept of mobility and utility. Based on a wheel hand trolley with wooden slats that fold away, the sunbed is both easy to transport and simple to understand. By adding a notch in one of the corners its functionality is furthered, creating the perfect holder for your bag while you rest. A Velcro strap can be added to secure the panels while wheeling the sunbed to your favourite location.

The sunbed gets its name from the town near Venice where the designer was born and where he spent part of his youth on the beach with his friends. The project reminds him of those times: 'For me the design of the bed is a project that is part of my best years, it is the place of the sun's journey of love but also to say goodbye. The sunbed at the beach has always conjured up the idea of a holiday which was then enriched with a broader meaning that is the discovery of life. The seascape, the sun, the beach, the beauty and youth that is soon gone. That memory of a sunset on the beach and being kissed by a last ray of sunshine.'

You will need:

Materials

_Hand trolley with two 260mm diameter pneumatic wheels, capacity 200kg

_Two wooden handles that fit the over frame. Beech is recommended.

_Two brass piano hinges, 20 x 500mm (parts C)

_Wood panel 25 x 1210 x 1210mm. Fir or birch plywood recommended.

_28 screws, 24 to attach the hinges, 4 longer screws to attach the frame to the plywood. These need to be long enough to go through the frame and into the board about two-thirds of the way.

Tools

_Drill

_Saw

1

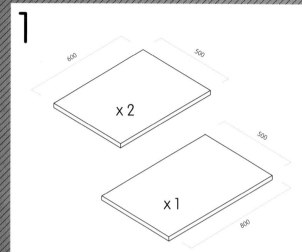

600
500

x 2

500

x 1

800

_Cut the wood panel into the following dimensions:
_Two boards of 25 x 500 x 600mm (part A)
_One board of 25 x 500 x 800mm (part B).

2

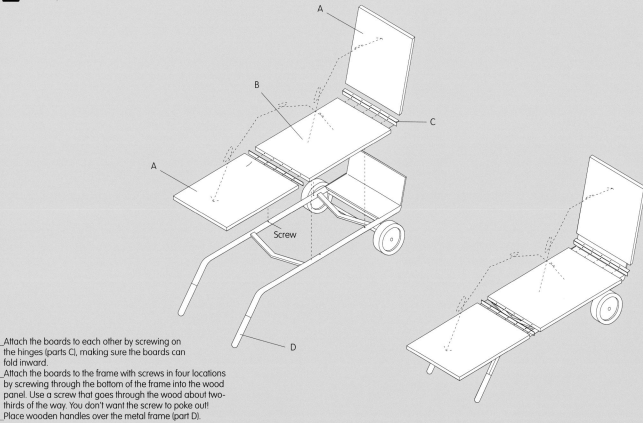

_Attach the boards to each other by screwing on the hinges (parts C), making sure the boards can fold inward.
_Attach the boards to the frame with screws in four locations by screwing through the bottom of the frame into the wood panel. Use a screw that goes through the wood about two-thirds of the way. You don't want the screw to poke out!
_Place wooden handles over the metal frame (part D).

3

_Wheel to your favourite spot and relax.

AMBIGUOUS CHAIR

ANNE-METTE MANELIUS

This chair has a structure that could only be cast in fabric formwork. It presents to the observer a physical object familiar in function and scale, but with ambiguous materiality and construction: there is a conflict between the appearance of the chair and the experience of touching it and sitting on it.

Fabric and a patterned or bulging surface are associated with upholstered furniture like Chesterfields, so it seemed a natural choice to use upholstery fabrics to cast a chair in concrete. By using fabrics to cast the chair, the designer has played on some of the associations that come with the function of a chair. Manelius writes: 'I've designed and produced chairs cast in fabric formwork in order to produce a structure which could only be cast in fabric, where I could explore if a surprise encounter with fabric-formed concrete can initiate curiosity and a dialogue with what concrete architecture could be.'

Architecture students at the University of Edinburgh studied the aesthetic surfaces of concrete cast in a number of conventional fabrics bought at the local fabrics store, including both very thin and cheap materials and more sturdy upholstery fabrics. By using upholstery fabric the pattern from the fabric transfers to the concrete surface, making the chair's appearance even more ambiguous to the observer.

The chair is cast in fibre-reinforced concrete. With flexible fabric formwork it was designed and produced as a thin, folding plane; the seat is sharply cantilevered and the surface is perforated for water to run off. This shell structure has created a fragile look not normally associated with concrete.

You will need:

Materials

_Three sheets plywood 18 x 900 x 900mm. Adjust for the size of your chair, they need to be a little larger than chair, but not too big.

_Six to eight pieces of wood 40 x 60mm, the width of your chair, minus two layers of plywood, in this case it is 564mm

_Screws 30mm and 70mm long

_72 bolts, 6mm diameter, 45–60mm long

_72 nuts 6mm

_72 lengths plastic plumbing pipe, 20mm diameter x 30mm long, total length 2500mm (or other tubing like copper – just keep in mind that it will remain visible after casting)

_140 metal washers, 15mm diameter with a 6mm hole. Here washers a little smaller than the tube are used. Washers larger than the tube will affect the cast.

_Five pieces of rebar, 6mm diameter, 2m long plus five pieces 550mm long. Steel grid could be a good alternative.

_Metal wire to tie the rebars together

_Fibre-reinforced, high-strength concrete, about 100 litres

_String, enough to measure the profile of the chair shape

_Plastic sheeting, enough to cover the form while the concrete is drying

_Sandpaper

_Hand lotion for dry skin

Tools

_Wrench and socket wrench

_Hammer

_Punch (awl)

_Ruler

_Small sharp knife

_Jigsaw

_4–8mm staples and a staple gun

_Power drill

_Shovel and bucket to mix concrete

_Protective equipment (breathing, eyes, ears, skin)

1

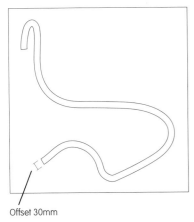

Offset 30mm

_Draw the profile shape of your chair onto a piece of plywood 900 x 900mm. Offset the line 30mm and draw it again.

2

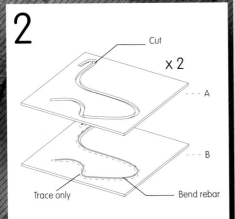

Cut

x 2

A

B

Trace only

Bend rebar

_Cut the shape out with a jigsaw and sand the edges. Repeat to make two pieces (parts A).
_Trace the shape onto the third piece of plywood, but don't cut it out. This will be a guide for placing screws later (part B).
_Bend a 2m-long rebar to the shape of your profile curve. Repeat so that you have two in total.

3

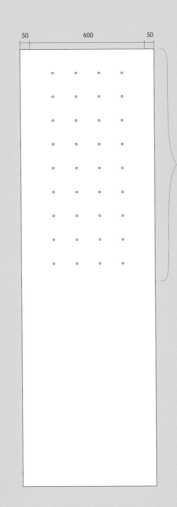

50   600   50

Grid half

_Cut the fabric to the width of the chair (in this case 600mm) and add 100mm, so here around 700mm.
_Use a string to measure the length of the profile curve. Double the length of the curve and add 200mm (you can stitch the pieces together).
_Make a pattern for your bolting area on the top half of the fabric. The piece shown here has a grid with 120mm spacing.
_Use an awl or the tip of a sharp knife to cut/punch holes for the bolts to fit through.

4

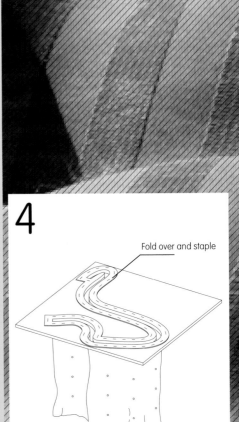

Fold over and staple

_Pull the end of the fabric through the chair-shaped hole and staple the edge of the fabric to the top of the board.

5

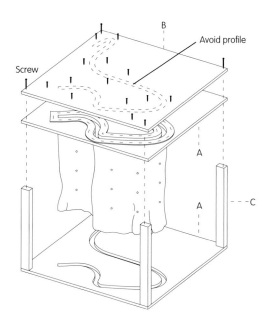

_Screw the third piece of plywood (part B) to part A, using the traced profile line as a guide to make sure you stay clear of the hole.
_Cut the 40 x 60mm struts (parts C) to the width of your chair minus 36mm (the thickness of two pieces of 18mm plywood).
_Attach the 40 x 60mm struts (parts C) between the two plywood pieces (parts A).
_Flip the form over.

6

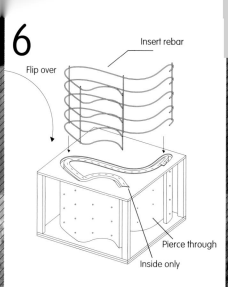

_Pull the fabric end through the other hole in the top piece of plywood and staple it to the top of the board. Only attach it to the inside curve for now.
_Complete the rebar assembly by attaching 550mm-long cross pieces to the profile pieces you bent in Step 1, using metal wire.
_Insert the rebar structure to add reinforcement.

7

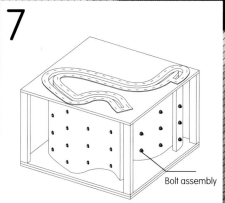

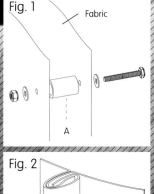

_Cut the 2500mm plastic pipe into 30mm pieces (part D) and insert them between the two sheets of fabric, clamping with the bolts, nuts, and washers. (see Fig. 1).
_Poke through the holes you have already punched and mark the other side of the fabric formwork. Then with a knife cut the opening of the holes just large enough to fit the bolt.
_Tighten the bolts. Ask a friend to hold one side while you tighten the nut with a socket wrench.
_Continue stapling the remaining fabric as you go.
_Connect the two ends of fabric by folding them over each other and attaching more bolt assemblies (see Fig. 2).
_Pour in the concrete.
_Cover the whole form with plastic sheeting and wait a minimum of 24 hours.

8

_Strip off the boards.
_With three friends (or a pallet truck) move your chair to your favourite spot.

_Concrete is a strongly alkaline material – protect your lungs and skin.
_Think your process backwards: you need to disassemble the formwork after the pour so don't put screws where you will later fill concrete!
_Cover screw heads with a big piece of tape to protect them from the concrete.
_For smaller concrete pieces, the spin cycle on your washing machine acts as a great vibration table to let excess air out of your mix.
_Fabric formwork can be compacted externally by pressing and massaging the concrete in place from the outside. Here a large vibration table was used, but rounded wooden sticks and your hands work well.
_The concrete is compacted when the fabric becomes wet on the outside. This means that there is a certain pressure in the form.
_Screw your formwork structure onto a pallet. Then you can move the filled piece easily with a pallet jack.

GREEN SCREEN

PAOLA DE FRANCESCO AND JOAO SILVA FOR
RECESSION DESIGN

This wooden plant screen is formed from simple wooden
shelving units, joined by aluminium corner pieces. You can also
use lightweight ladders joined in the same way. The screen can
be used both inside and out. Outside several screens joined
together become a pergola-like structure; inside they form
a room within a room.

The designers Paola De Francesco and Joao Silva, who are both
based in Milan, describe the screen as '… a house inside a
house. Where we can meet, we can work, we can eat, we can
transform, we can append, we can plant … we can do whatever!
And we can make it grow.'

You will need:

Materials

_Three units of wood side shelf 450 x
 2040mm (you can also use ladders)
 (part A)

_Three pieces of aluminium flat
 stock, 2 x 30 x 2000mm

_24 furniture connecting screws,
 (sleeve nuts) (part E)

_Plant containers with hanging
 brackets (part F)

Tools

_Handsaw for metal

_Drill

_Screwdriver

1

cut   cut   cut

550   C   C   550

30

B   450   450   B

x 2

_Using the handsaw, cut two pieces of aluminium flat stock in half so that there are four pieces 1000mm long.
_Divide each piece into a 550mm and a 450mm piece. The 550mm piece will be used for the round, external curve (part B) and the 450mm piece will be used for the internal curve of the metal structure (part C) that holds the top and the two legs of the screen.

2

cut   cut   cut

500   D   D   500

30

D   500   500   D

_Cut the remaining 2000m-long aluminium profile into four pieces each 500mm long. These will be used for the internal structure (part D) to maintain the shape.

3

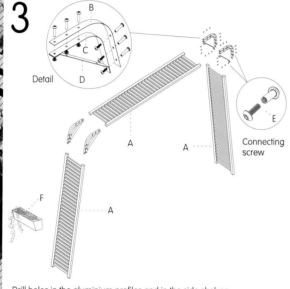

Detail

Connecting screw

_Drill holes in the aluminium profiles and in the side shelves for the screws. Use the same distance between all the holes in the aluminium profiles and the side shelves. In the example shown here the distance is 100mm.
_Connect the aluminium to the side shelves with the furniture screws (parts E).

4

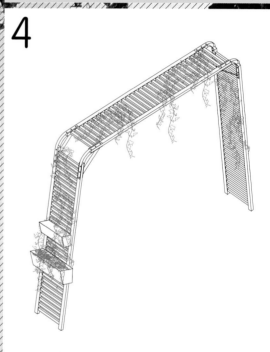

_Hang your plants in any way you like!

+

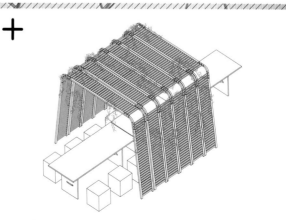

_Try combining several screens at once.

FIRE UP

EVELIEN STAMHUIS OF LIENEHUIS

Fire Up is a portable campfire in a bag. It's all you need to build a fire in no time.

The wooden struts are specially designed to optimize the starting of the fire. The six small kindling fire sticks are the first to burn; then six thicker blocks keep the fire going. These 12 wooden blocks are linked by a central circular piece that sits near the top of the construction.

The circular piece has holes in it that hold the main struts of the construction in position while the fire burns. The paper bag in which you carry Fire Up to your campfire location is used to start the fire when you arrive.

Just sit back and enjoy the outdoors. Create a special time with a special someone on the beach in the summer while the sun is going down. Or create some heat in the wintertime – with Fire Up you always have some dry wood. Now anyone can easily build a stylish campfire!

You will need:

Materials

_Pine plank 30 x 127 x 2000mm

_Pine plank 10 x 127 x 1500mm

_Pine board 15 x 250 x 250 mm

_Brown craft paper 180gsm, 350 x 1500mm

_A4 sticker

_Box of matches

Tools

_Jigsaw

_Scissors

_Glue for paper

1

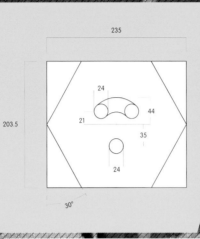
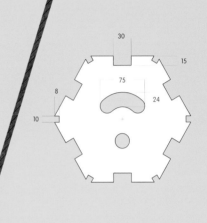

_Cut the centre connector from the 15 x 250 x 250mm board, as shown in the two diagrams.
_Start by cutting the sheet to 235 x 203.5mm. Then cut angles at 30 degrees.
_Drill three holes 24mm wide as shown, using a jigsaw to connect the two top circles with the two arched cuts as shown in the left-hand diagram.
_Then, cut the notches as shown in the right-hand diagram.

2

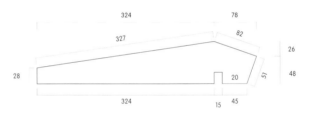

x 6

_Cut the large wooden struts from the 30 x 127 x 2000mm plank as shown in the diagram above.
_Repeat until you have six parts in total.

3

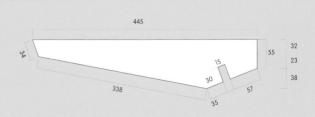

x 6

_Cut the small wooden struts from the 10 x 127 x 1500mm plank as shown in the diagram above.
_Repeat until you have six parts in total.

4

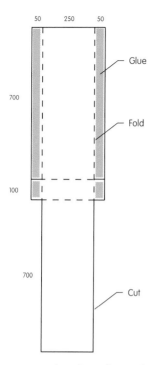

50 250 50

700

Glue

Fold

100

700

Cut

_Follow the measurements as shown above and use scissors to cut out the entire shape from the craft paper.
_Fold along the dotted lines, gluing where highlighted in grey.
_Place the wooden pieces in the bag with the box of matches and seal with the A4 sticker.
_Now your campfire kit is ready to use! Follow the remaining steps to assemble it.

5

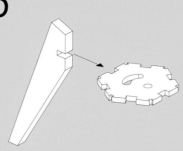

_Attach the six large wooden struts to the centre piece by sliding them into the large grooves.

6

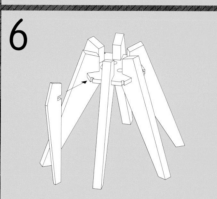

_Attach the six small wooden struts to the centre piece by sliding into the smaller grooves.

Fire up
camp fire

7

Tear

Fire up
camp fire

Light

_Tear the paper bag and use the paper as a starter for the fire by placing it inside the assembled campfire.

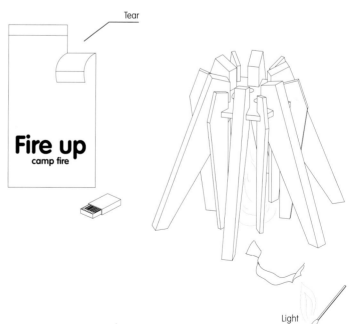

7.
MISC.

Accessorize, accessorize, accessorize! Even the nooks and crannies of your home need designer attention. On your way to the flea market, stop off at your local building supply store and pick up everyday materials that can be repurposed into uniquely designed accessories for your home. Cargo rope, copper and steel tubing, oak dowels, a light kit and an electrical socket are the bones for constructing some of the objects found in this chapter. A peek in the garage for some scrap wood, and a catalogue order will get you the rest of what you need to get started.

Whether you want a place to hang your hat, like on RBW's Coat Rack, or to bang your head to the sounds emanating from Symbiosis, a pair of mismatched speakers by Stanley Ruiz, this chapter is for you.

Rope in your nearest and dearest and get cosy on Supershape's superbly shaped rug. Change the playlist over to something more romantic, light the candles in Gylldorffs Vaudeville's holders and you will feel your hard work making furniture has paid off.

COAT RACK

RICH BRILLIANT WILLING

Rich Brilliant Willing aim to do more with less. As much artists as designers, they employ a gamut of tricks and techniques, from the magical to the scientific, to achieve extraordinary results.

They are an internationally renowned design studio and one of the most exciting firms currently working in the United States. They design at various scales from packaging and products to interior spaces and installations. Their methodology, evident in all their work, is a combination of technical sophistication with old-fashioned sleight of hand. They try to design new parts where necessary, or appropriate existing components and strategically rethink them. Their name is an example of this process, by re-imagining what was there to begin with – the three principal designers' names Richardson, Brill, Williams – combined into a single voice as Rich Brilliant Willing.

Their preferred definition of a designer is 'one who devises a course of action aimed at changing existing situations into preferred ones.' The result should always feel magically effortless but behind the curtain there is a laboratory hard at work; observation and analysis, hypothesis paired with experimentation, finally synthesis. It's a process of material and formal logic, with a refined aesthetic sensibility.

In keeping with their ethos of appropriation, RBW used ready-made catalogue parts like an industrial metal tripod to create this coat rack. The dimensions right are given in both millimetres for those using their own materials and inches for those sourcing them from the catalogue suggested by RBW.

You will need:

**Materials
from www.mcmaster.com**

_Tripod frame, suggest Mcmaster-Carr catalogue #8732T26 (includes crank)

_Alloy 932 bronze sleeve bearing, for 38mm (1½") shaft diameter, 102mm (4") long, suggest Mcmaster-Carr catalogue #6381k25 (part E)

_High-speed steel hardened oversized rod, 9.5mm (³⁄₈") diameter, 127mm (5") long, suggest Mcmaster-Carr catalogue #3023A236 (part A)

_Unthreaded thick-wall steel, seamless pipe, 6mm (¼") pipe size x 305mm (1') long, suggest Mcmaster-Carr catalogue #7972K112 (part C)

_PTFE-filled Delrin rod, 13mm (½") diameter, 305mm (1') long, suggest Mcmaster-Carr catalogue #8579K163 (part B)

_Copper tubing 9.5mm (³⁄₈") tube size, 13mm (½") external diameter, 9mm (³⁄₈") internal diameter, 16.5mm (⁵⁄₈") wall, 305mm (1') long, suggest Mcmaster-Carr catalogue #8967K362 (part D)

_Maple dowel rod 38mm (1½)" diameter, 1219mm (48") long, suggest Mcmaster-Carr catalogue #97015K25 (Part F)

_Coloured tape

_All-purpose glue

Tools

_Hacksaw

_Drill

_13mm and 9.5mm drill bits

1

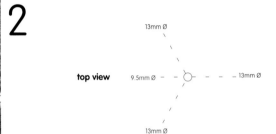

B — −200mm

C — −200mm

D — −200mm

F

A — − 127mm

— − 1219mm

_With the hacksaw cut 200mm of the following materials:
Delrin rod (part B)
Seamless pipe (part C)
Copper tubing (part D).
_A and F should already be to length. If not, cut A to
127mm and cut F to 1219mm.

2

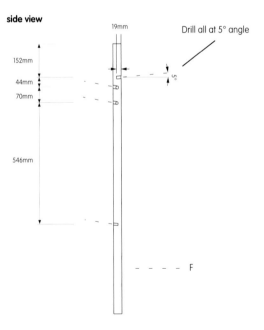

13mm Ø

top view   9.5mm Ø — ⊘ — − 13mm Ø

13mm Ø

side view

19mm

Drill all at 5° angle

152mm

44mm

70mm

5°

546mm

F

_Drill four holes into the maple dowel (part F) 19mm deep at
a 5-degree angle up from the horizontal. Mark your drill bit
with coloured tape so that you know how far to drill in. Use
a 13mm-diameter bit for the top three holes and
a 9.5mm-diameter bit for the lower hole.

3

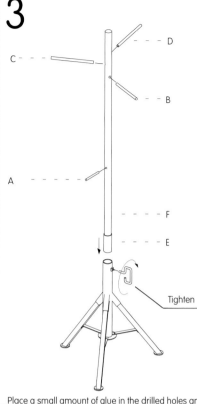

C ----- [rod]

D ----- D

B ----- B

A ----- A

F ----- F

E ----- E

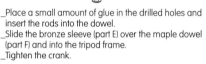
Tighten

_Place a small amount of glue in the drilled holes and insert the rods into the dowel.
_Slide the bronze sleeve (part E) over the maple dowel (part F) and into the tripod frame.
_Tighten the crank.

4

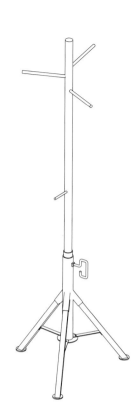

_Hang your coat and enjoy!

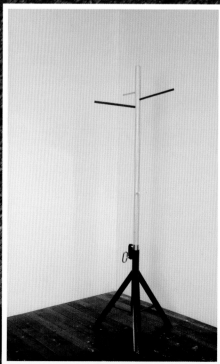

SAILOR'S DREAM

JONAS KLEIN OF SUPERSHAPE

Sailor's Dream is a rug made of 110 metres of heavy-duty cargo rope. By using common, existing materials that already have a purpose, Jonas Klein creates new pieces out of old materials, giving life to old objects and making us look at them in a new way.

The designer's aim was to create something very simple, an object that used as few different materials as possible. It was important that the object was useful, but at the same time displayed humour and irony; it was also important that it looked contemporary and that its purpose was clearly understood. Very thick rope in a mint green colour was used to make the carpet appear rough and iconic.

No specialized tools were used, just a rope, scissors and a lighter; then 110 metres of 40mm heavy-duty cargo rope and a roll of 3mm twine in the same colour to tie it together. The design uses a normal whip knot, which is easy to tie and holds the rug together extremely well. Both the colour and the thickness of the rope makes it a highly iconic design.

You will need:

Materials

_Roll of heavy-duty 40mm cargo rope, 110m long

_Roll of 3mm rope in the same colour

Tools

_Lighter

_Old knife

_Scissors

_Patience and time

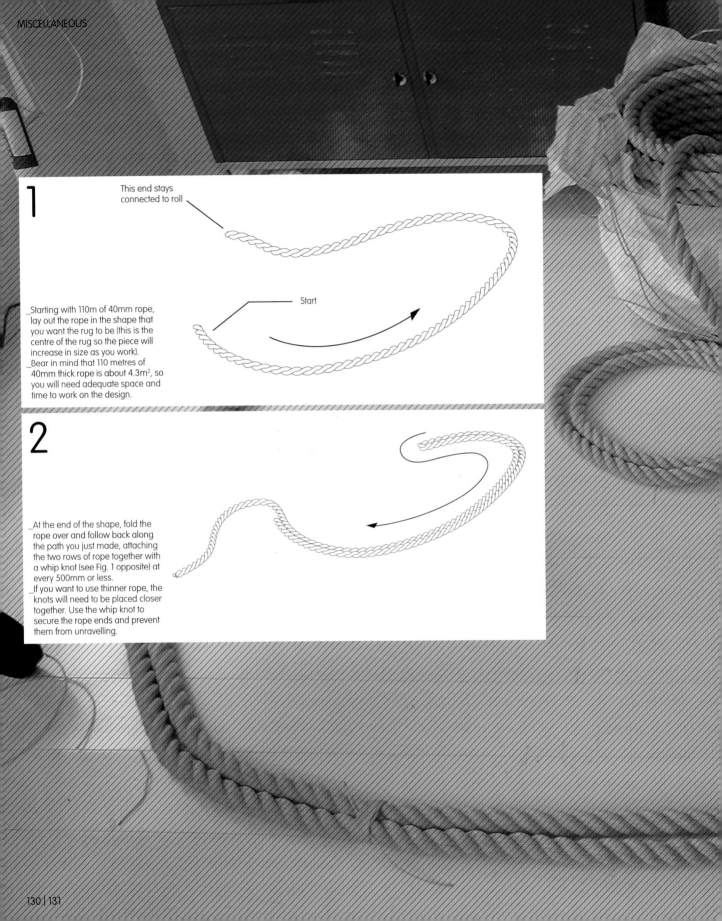

1

This end stays
connected to roll

Start

_Starting with 110m of 40mm rope,
lay out the rope in the shape that
you want the rug to be (this is the
centre of the rug so the piece will
increase in size as you work).
_Bear in mind that 110 metres of
40mm thick rope is about 4.3m^2, so
you will need adequate space and
time to work on the design.

2

_At the end of the shape, fold the
rope over and follow back along
the path you just made, attaching
the two rows of rope together with
a whip knot (see Fig. 1 opposite) at
every 500mm or less.
_If you want to use thinner rope, the
knots will need to be placed closer
together. Use the whip knot to
secure the rope ends and prevent
them from unravelling.

Fig. 1

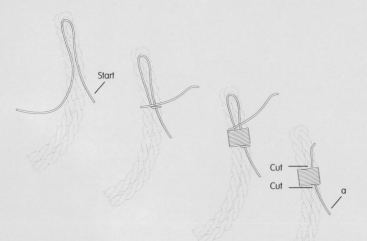

_Place the twine on the rope and make a loop.
_Wrap twine around the rope and over the loop.
_Repeat several times, then pull the twine through the loop.
_Pull the loop into the wrapped section by pulling on (a). Cut off
 the excess twine and melt the ends with the lighter to prevent
 them fraying.

3

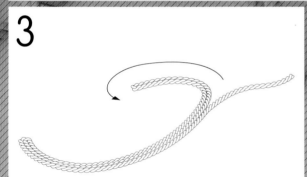

_Continue running the rope around the shape until you have
 the width of rug you require.

4

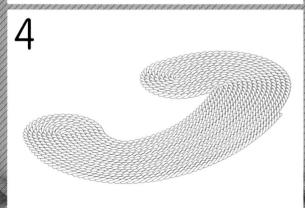

_Enjoy!

SYMBIOSIS WOOD SPEAKERS

STANLEY RUIZ

The designer Stanley Ruiz has an exploratory approach to design, combining natural materials with industrial ones like steel, and making this synthesis in an unusual and unexpected manner.

Symbiosis is a lo-fi approach to product design. Ruiz has improvised, using only found objects from his studio space like a tree log and scrap wood. He believes that product design should not be complicated, and not dependent upon the dictates of big marketing companies and manufacturers.

This work is an expressive design exploration that fulfils not only the function of regular speakers, but goes beyond that to include poetry, nature, folk inspiration, and intuition.

You will need:

Materials

_Two speakers (approx. 127mm diameter) with audio jack/ connectors

For log version

_Four 6mm metal rods, 914mm long (part A)

_Six 6–8mm oak dowels, 635–914mm long (part B)

_Log or tree branch, at least 25mm wider than speaker cone (here a 140mm-diameter x 508mm-long birch log)

_Cable ties

For scrap wood version

_Wood scraps, approx. 38–63mm x 343–406mm

_Four metal tubes 19mm square x 1219mm long (part C)

_Eight wooden dowels 10mm square, 305–406mm long (part D)

_Two pieces of MDF or plywood, roughly 280 x 280mm and 6–13mm thick

_Several small nails and a few small screws

_Cable ties

_Four carriage bolts, wing nuts, 6mm diameter, 38mm long

_Wood glue

_Steel wool and acetone (optional)

Tools

_Drill

_Chisel

_Hammer

_Saw

_Jigsaw

_Soldering gun

_Stanley knife or cutting pliers

Log version

Select appropriate speakers (here Joey Roth's ceramic speakers), then look for a suitable log/tree branch.

1

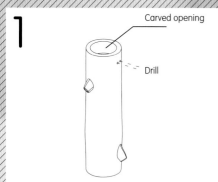

Carved opening

Drill

_Cut or carve an opening on one end of the log to accommodate the speaker cone (here a power drill, a chisel and a hammer were used).
_Drill two small holes to mount the jacks/connectors.

2

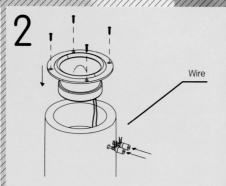

Wire

_Wire the speakers to the jacks/connectors by soldering them together.
_Screw the speaker into place from the front side.

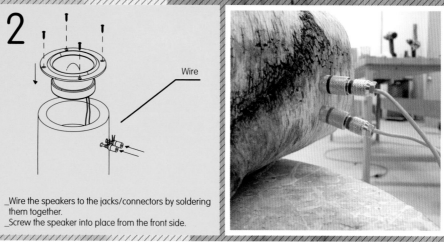

3

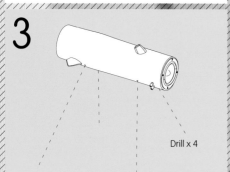

Drill x 4

_Drill four 6mm-diameter holes about 50–76mm deep in the log at the desired angle for the legs. Make sure the holes are drilled far enough away from the speaker housing. About 127mm from the end is good.

4

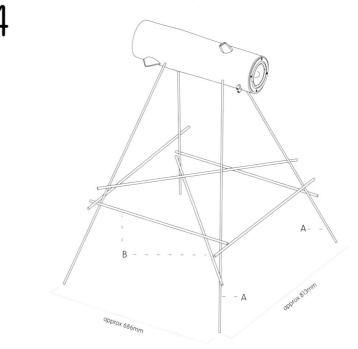

A

B

A

approx 686mm

approx 813mm

_Use off-the-shelf components to construct the base. In this case, 6mm-diameter raw steel (parts A) was used with round 6–8mm oak dowels (parts B).
_Secure the structure with cable ties. Make an x shape with two ties for extra strength (see Fig. 1). Trim off any excess with the Stanley knife.
_To make the unit more stable add additional dowel cross-bracing as necessary.

Fig. 1

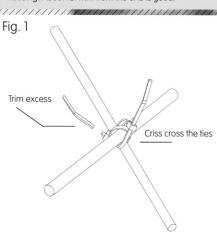

Trim excess

Criss cross the ties

Scrap wood version

Collect various types of scrap wood in different thicknesses.

1

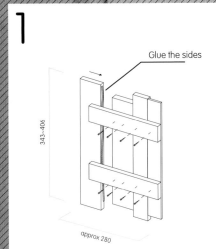

Glue the sides

343–406

approx 280

_Build a box baffle using scrap pieces of wood (38–63mm) by gluing them sideways.
_Reinforce the box with (scrap wood) cross-pieces. Use nails or screws as necessary.

2

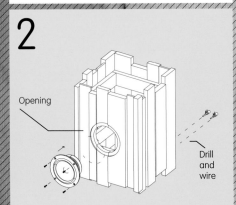

Opening

Drill and wire

_Using a jigsaw, cut a circular opening approximately 25mm less than the diameter of the speaker cone.
_If your scrap pieces are different thicknesses, you will need to carve a flat spot with a chisel the diameter of the speaker.
_Screw the speakers onto the front side of the scrap wood box.
_Drill two small holes at the back panel to mount the audio jacks.
_Mount the jacks/connectors and solder the wiring. It is easier to solder at this point than when the box is mounted on the legs.

3

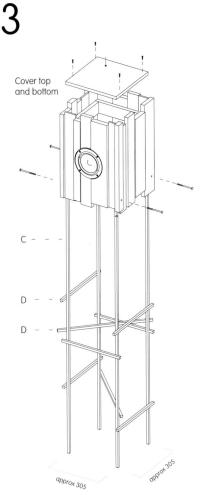

Cover top and bottom

C

D

D

approx 305   approx 305

_Close the top and bottom of the box with MDF or plywood (use screws so that you can get to the speakers if you need to repair them).
_Construct the legs using unfinished 19mm square steel tube (parts C) and 10mm square wood dowels (parts D) secured with cable ties (see Fig. 1 opposite).
_Clean the raw metal with fine steel wool and a little solvent (e.g. acetone).
_Set the box on the base and drill four 6mm-diameter holes through the sides of the box and the four metal legs.
_Secure the box with four carriage bolts and wing nuts.

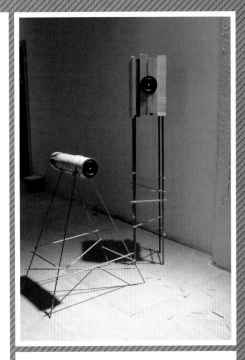

4

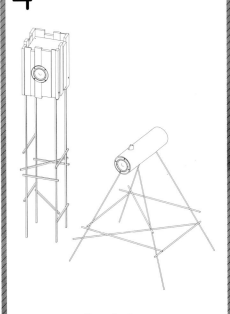

_Plug in to the amplifier and rock out!

LJUSSTAKE CANDLE HOLDERS

MATS GYLLDORFF OF GYLLDORFFS VAUDEVILLE

Use less electricity. That was the designer's first thought when he came up with the Ljusstake Candle Holders. Instead of lighting up your room with electricity, use old-fashioned candlelight.

Gylldorff uses bendable cords a lot when sketching in 3D and one day when working on a light project at university he sat with lamp sockets of different sizes. Taking a break from the project, he began to make different shapes with the cord. At the time he was looking for a candle holder for personal use. Suddenly it occurred to him that the size of the lamp holder was the same diameter as that of a candle. And so through playfulness and sketching the Ljusstake was born.

Gylldorff used the bendable electrical cord and formed it into a stand shape. Then he added an old lamp socket and holder to make it look like it was a real electrical device. The aim was to make people reflect on the amount of unnecessary energy they use. By putting a candle in what seems to be a cord for lamps you get an immediate reaction.

You will need:

Materials

_EKLK electrical cord, around 1m long (use the cord wire that stays rigid when you bend it)

_Electrical socket

_Lamp holder

_Candle

_Matches

_Super glue

Tools

_Pliers

_Stanley knife

1

Cut

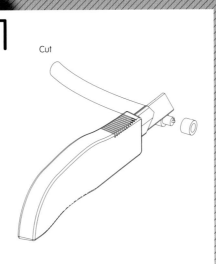

_Use the pliers to cut the cord into a 1m length.
_With the Stanley knife cut off the first layer from one end of the cord (as shown in Fig. 1, above right). This is where you will attach the lamp holder.
_At the other end, cut off all the layers except the three inner cords (as shown in Fig. 1, in the lower example). This is where you will attach the socket.

2

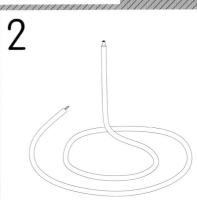

_Shape the cord into the form that you want.

3

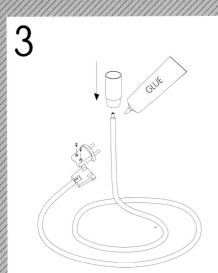

GLUE

_Apply some glue to the lampholder and screw it onto the wire.
_Apply glue to the other end of the cord if necessary. Screw the electrical socket to the cord.

4

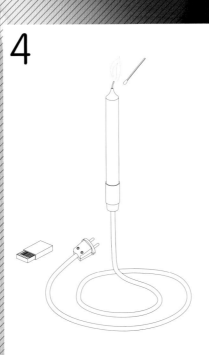

_Insert the candle and light it.

Lindsey Adams Adelman and Bec Brittain – Lindsey Adelman Studio

Born in New York City in 1968 Lindsey Adams Adelman currently lives in Brooklyn, NY. Inspired by her work at the Smithsonian, she studied industrial design at Rhode Island School of Design. An ongoing interest in combining the hand-crafted with the machine-made, the sensual with the practical, and the feminine with the masculine consistently marks her work. Adelman founded the company Butter with David Weeks in 2000 where they designed affordable products for the home until 2005. Since then Adelman has focused on her own line of hand-blown glass lighting. Her collective work has been included in the Cooper-Hewitt Design Triennial and Design Miami.

Bec Brittain is a designer and artist in Brooklyn. After studying furniture design and then graduating in philosophy from NYU, Brittain received an architecture degree from the Architectural Association in London. Her work consistently reflects her variety of interests by creating relationships between normally disparate elements. Brittain has been Design Director at Lindsey Adelman Studio since 2008.

www.lindseyadelman.com

Luca Buttafava and Alessandro Confalonieri – INTERSEZIONI Design Studio

Luca Buttafava and Alessandro Confalonieri are directors of the INTERSEZIONI design consultancy based in Milan, where they create products and integrated services, incorporating knowledge of user needs and wishes to generate strategies and develop new projects. They design ad-hoc workshops for companies and organizations to facilitate and speed up the approach to their final product. Current clients include Apam, Atm, Autogrill, Ferrero, Nestlé, Papaiz.

www.intersezioni.net

Jae Won Cho – J1studio

Founder and designer at J1studio Jae Won Cho was born in South Korea and moved to the United States at the age of 16, where he became interested in sculpture and architecture. After graduating from Art Center College of Design, with a Bachelor of Science degree in environmental design, he started an experimental design studio based in Los Angeles, focusing on furniture and temporary spaces. The studio produces simple, unique, modular objects and systems that have the quality of sculpture but function as furniture.

www.J1studio.com

Paola De Francesco & Joao Silva – Defrancesco+Silva Studio

Paola De Francesco was born in Milan and graduated in architecture from the city's university in 1996; Joao Silva was born in Faro, Portugal, and graduated in design from the Politecnico di Milano in 1996 and in architecture in 2000. Together the pair founded Defrancesco+Silva Studio in 2004. Based in Milan, the studio works across the whole range of design and architecture, designing the Milanese concept fashion store PHCY, the Don Peperone restaurant chain and the office furniture line Fluido for the Turkish company ERSA. In 2009 they embraced the birth of the Recession Design group and from that time have participated in all the RD exhibitions. Their work is included in the permanent collection at the MAK Vienna, the Austrian Museum of Applied Arts/Contemporary Art.

www.defrancescosilva.com

Luigi Fumagalli

Born in 1970 in Mariano Comense (CO), Italy, Fumagalli graduated in architecture from the Politecnico di Milano in 1997; one year later he obtained his professional qualification in architecture. In 1997 he began a collaboration with the Ambrosini Miyajima architectural practice based in Como, where he was responsible for designing the showrooms of many famous Italian fashion brands all over Italy and Europe. He has worked at Cibic&Partners architectural practice in Milan since 2000 and has collaborated in planning and designing many remarkable projects, among them the 10th International Architectural Exhibition in Venice in 2006. Along with his role within the practice, he also takes on private professional commissions.

www.recessiondesign.org

William Gittins

Living in Colombia between 2005 and 2008 Gittins was influenced by what he saw as chance 'defining the daily unpredictable patterns of life'. Within this environment he produced a distinct body of work and formed a studio. Having studied and worked as a designer in London, his direction in Colombia was defined by 'an opportunity for independent creativity in an irregular local infrastructure'.

He was also influenced by the need to keep the use of technology to a minimum, a need compensated by a culture of hand forming and recycling materials. Recycling in Colombia is not only part of the informal economy but a last chance for survival for the many who live in a marginalized subculture.

In London Gittins' output is broader, working to a brief and with access to more technologies. His self-initiated projects tend to focus on simplifying processes and 'exploring the associated characteristics of the structural patterns that surround us'.

www.williamgittins.com

Nicola Golfari

Born in 1969 in the Barro Mountain region near Lake Como, Golfari began thinking about design through observing nature and dismantling toys and devices. After graduating from the Politecnico di Milano in architecture and design, he started working in several studios, including Cibic&Partners, where he worked on interior and retail design projects and got to know 'a lot of smart and special people'. In 1999, with Zoran and Dragana Minic, he founded POP SOLID studio, working on product design and interior architecture until 2009. In 2010 he founded panicdesign.it studio, working on architecture, product design and as a consultant for retail design projects.

Golfari is one of the co-founders of the Recession Design group. The aim of the group is to make objects with materials that are easily available in DIY shops, using everyday tools and accessories. Their simplicity and clean lines are the proof that good design can result from easily sourced materials and utensils, without resorting to special materials or technology. The idea behind Recession Design is very simple but opens an interesting debate on the meaning of design today: the economic crisis provides an opportunity for critical reflection on the contemporary design world. The 'DIY design' philosophy proposes a clean and simple 'design' method that returns the object's pure form and function to the centre of the design process, going beyond the trends of the moment and liberating the design process from limits imposed by overly complex technologies.

www.recessiondesign.org

Mats Gylldorff – Gylldorffs Vaudeville

Born in 1981, designer and illustrator Gylldorff lives in Stockholm and founded Gylldorff & Svalin with a colleague, at the beginning of 2009 and ran it for almost two years. They exhibited products around Europe at different design fairs, such as imm Cologne, Stockholm Furniture Fair and DMY Berlin. Gylldorff moved to Stockholm in the autumn of 2010 and now runs his own creative bureau called Gylldorffs Vaudeville, which focuses on design and illustration. He has studied design and art in Florence, Italy, and in the dark forests of Sweden. His other interests besides design and illustration include moustaches.

www.gylldorffsvaudeville.com

Jonas Klein – Supershape

Danish designer Jonas Klein finds inspiration from the most unexpected sources, and has a predilection for simple shapes. They give tranquility and simplicity to his design. His works are characterized by a simplicity that comes from a primary idea about function. Klein often begins with a pattern, a system or a particular shape that gradually, and in part unconsciously, develops and takes shape, eventually becoming a design that evolves through several prototypes. In the past few years, he has also worked with objects and projects located in the borderland between design and art. His carpet, Sailor's Dream, is an example of this.

www.supershape.org

Gabriela Kowalska – KOFIKOLEKTIF

At the beginning of 2009 two young designers, Gabriela Kowalska and Krzysztof Filipczyk created the design studio KOFIKOLEKTIF. Through quality, ergonomics and unique style KOFIKOLEKTIF's aim is to change forever the space around us. Their designs focus on creatively employing already 'used' materials/products and those not usually associated with design. They like to play with context, giving another meaning to their work. KOFIKOLEKTIF's concern for the environment leads it to explore every area of production in order to create eco-smart, high-quality products. In 2010, Gabriela started Gabukow, where she continues her work.

www.gabukow.pl

Florian Kräutli

Kräutli was born in 1985 in Winterthur, Switzerland. After his first year at art school in Lucerne he begain studying at the 'Man & Living' department at the Design Academy Eindhoven in the Netherlands. In 2008 he received a rabbit with a silver ear. On graduation in 2009 he received a bunch of carrots. In 2009 he received the federal design award of Switzerland, his first award that did not consist of food or animals! In his work he likes to play. Playing is for him a way of exploring possibilities. He describes it as 'using a spoon as a catapult, a plate as a frisbee, a bed as a fortress. It is a means of finding out things I wouldn't be able to imagine.'

www.kraeutli.com

Sarah Kueng and Lovis Caputo – Kueng Caputo

Sarah Kueng and Lovis Caputo live and work in Zürich. They began their collaboration in 2006 and graduated in product design from the Hochschule für Gestaltung Zürich. Under the name of Kueng Caputo, their work proposes an ironic and playful approach to daily life. They have realized innovative projects such as Five Star Cardboard and Copy by Kueng Caputo, exploring mundane materials and environments to exercise and reflect high design/architectural concepts. They especially like to work on given circumstances and they love to analyse the facts till they can figure out a surprising, simple solution. Kueng Caputo have exhibited at museums, galleries and design/art fairs worldwide, including venues in Zürich, Basel, Milan, Cape Town, Seoul, Osaka, Tokyo and New York.

www.kueng-caputo.ch

Paul Loebach

Loebach received a Bachelor of Fine Arts in industrial design from Rhode Island School of Design in 2002 and moved to New York immediately after graduating to found his furniture and product design office. He now works as a designer and manufacturing consultant with a broad range of American and European furniture companies, with over 200 designs currently in production. Loebach's projects have become widely recognized for their ability to explore the relationship between craft, technology, and the history of our manufactured environment. His work and writing has been exhibited internationally and published broadly in books, weblogs, and periodicals such as: *Wallpaper*, Surface, I.D., Interior Design, Elle Decor UK, Architectural Record* and *The New York Times*, among many others.

www.paulloebach.com

Julia Lohmann

Julia Lohmann is a London-based designer interested in unusual and undervalued natural and man-made materials. Lohmann probes our attitudes towards the world that sustains us. Her work is exhibited worldwide and is part of major private and public collections, such as the MoMA, New York. She teaches at the Royal College of Art in London and in 2008 was selected as one of four 'Designers of the Future' by Design Miami.

 www.julialohmann.co.uk.

MALAFOR

MALAFOR are Polish husband and wife duo Agata Kulik and Pawel Pomorski. Pomorski studied industrial design at the Academy of Fine Arts in Gdansk, Poland, and created MALAFOR in 2004. The couple started creating objects that could be produced in short bursts (such as Newspaper Table and Pipe Line Shelf). They are now also working on industrial design projects, such as Active Basket – a shopping basket for people in wheelchairs – and household projects commissioned by external companies. They are winners of several awards, including the Grand Prix at the Targetti Light Art Award in Florence, Italy, in 2006 and the Grand Prix at the NAGOYA DESIGN DO!, Japan, in the same year. They often like to include humour and a second meaning in their work.

www.malafor.com

Anne-Mette Manelius

Born in 1976, Manelius is an architect living and working in Copenhagen. She holds a Masters in Architecture from the Royal Danish Academy of Fine Arts in Copenhagen (RDAFA) and is currently working on her industrial PhD project about the architectural potential of fabric formwork for concrete structures. Fabric formwork is a new building technology in which flat sheets of woven textiles can be used as lightweight and flexible formwork for casting concrete structures. It offers the potential to produce advanced geometric structures, which can be tailor-made in simple fabrics. The technique can be used to cast slender design pieces, robust building structures, and for infrastructural solutions. The practice-based thesis work is done at RDAFA and sponsored by the Ministry of Science, Technology and Innovation, and in affiliation with the architectural office schmidt/hammer/lassen and contractor E. Pihl & Son.

www.concretely.blogspot.com

Peter Marigold

Peter Marigold is a London-based furniture designer. Working directly with materials, he approaches furniture design as a formal sculptural activity, producing designs for both mass production and galleries. His work is exhibited widely including at the Milan Furniture Fair, Design Miami, Stavanger 2008 (Norway), MoMA New York and 21_21 Design Sight, Tokyo.

After graduating from the Royal College of Art in 2006 his exhibition at the Design Museum in London was awarded an Esmée Fairburn bursary that enabled him to establish his design studio and workshop. In 2009 he was awarded one of the four 'Designer of the Future' awards by Design Miami, and is currently working with Murray Moss in New York.

www.petermarigold.com

MOOMOO Architects

MOOMOO Architects was founded in 2008 by Jakub Majewski and Lukasz Pastuszka. In 2009 *Wallpaper** magazine selected the practice as one of the best 30 young offices in the world. Their work has been shown in exhibitions in London, Shanghai, Rotterdam and Brussels.

www.moomoo.pl

Marissa Morelli

Born in the Netherlands in 1967 and now based in Milan, Morelli studied at the Politecnico di Milano and the University of Florence. She has worked with Claudio Nardi (www.claudionardi.it), Claudio Silvestrin (www.claudiosilvestrin.com) and Aldo Cibic (www.cibicpartners. com) and has freelanced on various personal projects. Interior architecture and design are the main fields in which she has developed her experience, taking project designs from first concept through detailed design stages and on to project management.

She has been part of the Recession Design design team since its foundation.

WOM/working on memory is Morelli's project with photographer Max Rommel, which investigates lack of memory in landscapes, architecture and people.

www.workingonmemory.com

Theo Richardson, Charles Brill and Alexander Williams – Rich Brilliant Willing

Rich Brilliant Willing are Theo Richardson, Charles Brill and Alexander Williams. Founded in 2007, Rich Brilliant Willing is an internationally recognized multidisciplinary design studio.

Why do they work together? The combined output is greater than the sum of individual parts. Each member has a different point of view; one explicitly loves materiality; another has an unconventional colour palette and eye for sculptural form; the third is an inventor bringing spontaneity and theatrical energy to the work.

The studio's work has a unique expression. It's about materials used in exciting ways, about sculptural and proportional relationships; it's an additive process that is never decorative. They riff on bringing the abstract simplicity of manufactured components into a domestic context. Industrial paint finishes are used for their eccentric colour palette and durability, hardwoods offer a warmth not found in metal or other options, and the list goes on. Each decision represents an economical and feasible logic. The studio has a commitment to innovation, and is inspired by practical solutions. The output feels like a celebratory vision of working within constraints, rather than being bound by them.

Accolades have since been received by the Manhattan-based office: Rich Brilliant Willing was named among the Top 40 designers by *I.D.* magazine in January 2009, and named an Avant Guardian by *Surface* magazine in November of the same year. With recent press including major publications such as *FRAME, Metropolis, Architecture Moniteur* and multiple appearances in *the New York Times,* their notoriety continues to grow.

www.richbrilliantwilling.com

Max Sanjulian – Volido

Volido is lead by Max Sanjulian and from its bases in Manhattan and Barcelona operates responsibly in the context of contemporary urban culture. The studio works across urban planning and industrial design in what Sanjulian describes as 'a competitive combination of traditional old school practice, American pragmatism and emotional personal expression … all dressed in a post-punk mood without complexes. Using economy as the main conceptual currency, new complexities, new standards and sustainability are variables that are addressed from the austerity of one solution without options, rejecting the 90's wide-angle-big-wallet idea everything is possible. In an old-fashioned way Volido survives, avoiding clients that have lost the desire to crystallize in their own world … and works for free men and free women, or for the ones not yet free but with a strong desire for freedom. Not to be read as pure manifesto but as a marketing strategy. In Volido we love Freedom and Freedom could be profitable.'

www.volido.com

Evelien Stamhuis – Lienehuis

Stamhuis was born in 1985 at Stadskanaal in the Netherlands and graduated from the Artez Institute of Arts, Arnhem, the Netherlands in 2009. She established Lienehuis in 2009, which is also based in Arnhem. In her designs Stamhuis aims to create straightforward products. How they are used and, especially the interaction between the design and the user, is very important to her. She likes to make you look again at the objects that surround you. In 2010 she exhibited Fire Up at Ambiente Frankfurt. Together with Temporary Collective Arnhem she also exhibited at DMY Berlin 2010.

www.lienehuis.nl

Stanley Ruiz

Stanley Ruiz is a product designer with an extensive background in craft design and production. In his works, he fuses the industrial with the natural to bring about new meaning and interpretation to familiar object archetypes. Based in Brooklyn, NY, he was born in Manila, and for several years lived in Bali where he worked in traditional handicrafts.

www.stanleyruiz.com

Maria Cristina Rueda and Leah Reyes – Uhuru Design

Uhuru is a sustainable design-and-build furniture company based in Red Hook, Brooklyn. Responsible for the design of the Warehouse Vanity, Maria Cristina Rueda and Leah Reyes make up part of Uhuru. Rueda was born and raised in Bogotá, Colombia and attended Parsons School of Design in New York. She is a multidisciplinary designer with experience and interest in different mediums like print, type, branding, layout, installations, exhibitions and events. Born in San Diego, California, Reyes graduated from Philadelphia University. She has a background in both interior and furniture design, and finds inspiration in writing and creating around Brooklyn.

www.uhurudesign.com

Cristiano Urban

Having graduated from the Faculty of Architecture in Venice, Urban began collaborating with Aldo Rossi in 1991, first as a photographer, for which he developed a passion. He then worked as an architect. In 2000 he started a working relationship with Aldo Cibic and he still collaborates with Cibic&Partners on interior design. He has concrete experience with projects such as Pocket's landscape design, with research topics related to a new concept of living with nature. Currently, he is working with the consultants H16 who have developed a project of mobile homes, experimenting with new housing solutions. These are living spaces where functions are reduced to the essentials, based on the real needs of the individual, thus eliminating unnecessary needs dictated by today's society.

www.cristianourban.com

Jorre van Ast

Prior to attending the Royal College of Art, London, van Ast had a background in industrial design. He studied industrial product design at The Hague University of Applied Sciences and worked at design studio Flex in the Netherlands. After graduating from the RCA Design Products course in 2006, he worked as an independent designer, sharing a collective studio in North London, known as OKAY studio (www.okaystudio.org) where he focused on (interior) product design. OKAY studio is not an organized company or brand. Its members do not strictly design together nor necessarily even work together. They were brought together by a simple common goal to share a space in which their creativity can flourish and build upon each others' knowledge and skills. Besides his personal work, van Ast has recently joined contemporary furniture manufacturer Arco (www.arco.nl) in the Netherlands, where he is Creative Director.

Although generally functionally orientated, his work has an additional layer that could be loosely defined as the 'informal' element. Through this juxtaposition of opposing concerns he tries to uncover new and playful typologies. By manipulating 'principals', and pushing the nature of what we consider to be normal in a material or an object, he hopes to add a new meaning and interpretation that goes beyond the expected and purely utilitarian.

www.jorrevanast.com

Erwin Zwiers

Erwin Zwiers was born in 1983 in Castricum, a small town near Amsterdam, where he still lives. It is near the woods and the North Sea, which is a very inspiring place for him and where he indulges his passion – kite surfing. After studying cabinet making and 3D-product design, Zwiers started his own design studio, Studio Erwin Zwiers in 2009. He designs interiors and interior products and also produces them. Zwiers experiments a lot with different materials for new products and tries to exploit a material's qualities so that the most simple materials can be used to create the most beautiful forms or new techniques.

www.erwinzwiers.nl

Acknowledgements

I would first like to thank all of the contributing desigers for supplying me with such amazing work and for being patient during the many demands required of them. Your creative minds are an inspiration. A special thanks to Laurence King Publishing and Editorial Director Jo Lightfoot for believing in this book and for giving me my first opportunity as an author. Thank you Peter Jones, Senior Editor, and Jon Allan at TwoSheds Design for understanding and adding to my vision with the execution of this book and its design.

This book is dedicated to my loving wife Rachel and cohorts that believed in me and put up with my absence while I spent countless hours in the shop and in front of the computer! Thanks for your loving support.

Photography

Robin Grann: pages 136, 137
Julia Lohmann: pages 21, 22, 23
Peter Marigold: pages 5 (storage), 38, 39, 40, 41
Justin Marr / Le Beouf blog: www.blog.unit3a.nu: page 61
Michelle Pemberton / Red Rocket Studio: pages 66, 80, 81, 84 (middle right, bottom right and background), 85 (bottom right)
Max Rommel: pages 5 (bedroom), 69, 77, 93, 109, 116, back cover (middle left and bottom right)
Morgan Satterfield / The Brick House blog: www.the-brick-house.com: back cover (bottom left)
J. Stelmaszek / Grappa Studio: pages 29, 30, 31
Soomee Vert: pages 6, 13, 14, 15 (top right)
Cho Yoon-Jong: front cover, pages 26, 42, 43, 44, 45

Illustration

Lindsey Adelman Studio: pages 62, 63, back cover (middle right)
Jae Won Cho: page 45 (cable tie detail)
Malafor: pages 10, 11, 47

Petralito Rotiroti Associati: pages 32 (top right), 35 (bottom right assembled view), 70 (top right), 71 (exploded view, assembled view and cable tie detail), 79 (exploded view and assembled view), 92 (top), 108 (background), 111 (exploded view and assembled view), 117 (middle row and bottom right)

Additional credits

Ambiguous Chair
Assistant: BA student in Architectural Engineering Jannie Bakkœr Sørensen. Consultants: Technical University of Denmark, Dep. of Civil Engineering.
Industrial partners of the PhD project for which the work was done: E. Pihl & Son, and Schmidt Hammer Lassen Architects.
Academic part of the PhD: The Royal Danish Academy of Fine Arts, School of Architecture, Institute of Technology, Centre for Industrialized Architecture.

Box Sideboard
Text written in collaboration with Maria Garcia

KOFITABLE
Built by Gabriela Kowalska and Krysztof Filipczyk

Recession Design (Divano Letto Sofabed, Green Screen, Jesolo Sunbed, Poltrona Armchair, Sedia E Sgabello, Writing Desk)
Art direction: POP Solid

Symbiosis Wood Speakers
Fabrication/Production: Stanley Ruiz
Original Speaker used: Ceramic Speaker by Joey Roth
Produced for Sounds Like, an ICFF offsite exhibition curated by Joey Roth (May 2010, New York)

The Panther
Collaborators: Marco Roso, Angela Hau, Fabia Lukowski, Charles Kettaneh, Nicolas Moussallem, Nathalie Schwer

Warehouse Vanity
Special thanks from Bill Hilgendorf and Jason Horvath to the Uhuru Team

About the Author

Before books and objects, Christopher Stuart began as an artist, primarily oil painting. His work has won numerous awards and has been exhibited in some of the top galleries in the US, as well as featured in many leading art magazines. Later, his focus turned to industrial design where his love for 3D and functional objects developed. While honing his design skills as Lead Industrial Designer for Thomson Consumer Electronics (GE and RCA Brand), he was also developing his skills as a sculptor and sharing his painting knowledge as an instructor at various art centres. After Thomson, Chris was able to continue innovating for big brands, working at a consultancy in Atlanta.

In 2007, Chris founded Luur, a multidisciplinary design studio that combined his experience as a designer and as an artist. Luur Studio takes a unique, empathetic approach to design by finding and building emotional connections between the object and the user. Luur Studio discovers ways to not only marry form and function, but to seamlessly bridge them and use each as an opportunity to springboard in the design process. Today, through Luur Studio, Chris continues to work with big brands and start-ups while also developing self-initiated projects in furniture and accessories. Keeping in spirit with his tenacious hunger to grow and try new things, he went on to author this book as a way to share his and like-minded others' creative design solutions.

www.luurdesign.com